THE COOK'S
HERB
GARDEN

Jeff Cox & Marie-Pierre Moine

London, New York, Melbourne, Munich, and Delhi

Editors Helena Caldon,
Constance Novis
Photographers William Reavell,
Peter Anderson, Sarah Ashun

Project Editor Andrew Roff
Project Designer Will Hicks
Designer Elly King
Managing Editors Dawn Henderson,
Angela Wilkes
Managing Art Editor Christine Keilty
Senior Jacket Creative Nicola Powling
Senior Production Editor Jennifer Murray
Senior Production Controller Seyhan Esen
Creative Technical Support Sonia Charbonnier

First published in Great Britain in 2010
by Dorling Kindersley Limited
80 Strand, London WC2R 0RL

Penguin Group (UK)

Copyright © 2010 Dorling Kindersley Limited
Text copyright © 2010 Dorling Kindersley Limited

2 4 6 8 10 9 7 5 3 2 1

A CIP catalogue record for this book is available
from the British Library

ISBN 978-1-4053-4993-2

Colour reproduction by Colourscan, Singapore

Printed and bound by
Hung Hing Printing Group Ltd., China

Discover more at
www.dk.com

*DK would like to thank
Petersham Nurseries
for their beautiful planted
pots and baskets.*

www.petershamnurseries.com

CONTENTS

4   Introductions

 CHOOSE

7   Planted Pots and Baskets
20 The Herb Catalogue

 GROW

76 Climate
80 Planning
84 Soil
86 Growing from Seed
88 Growing Young Plants
90 Propagating
92 Feeding and Watering
94 Weed Control
96 Improving your Harvest
98 Pests
100 Diseases

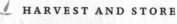 **HARVEST AND STORE**

104 Reaping the Harvest
108 Short-term Storage
110 Freezing
114 Drying

 COOK

122 Preparation
128 Flavourings
130 The Recipes
178 Herbal Teas
186 Partner Charts

190 Index
192 Acknowledgments

A NOTE FROM THE GARDENER JEFF COX

I always think of culinary herbs as the champions of the kitchen garden. Their volatile oils – so attractive in teas and as flavours in our cooking – evolved as compounds plants use to defend themselves from insects and fungi. Both cooks and gardeners therefore benefit from a herb's aromas, because you don't need to use environmentally disruptive chemicals to protect them.

As I work and live with herbs, I befriend them. The familiar perennials return year after year to greet me with each warming spring; while the new annual acquaintances, which need sowing every year, unfurl from their tiny seeds into replicas of herbs from last year. Every year and throughout the seasons, the herb garden returns this friendship with a feast for all the senses.

In my garden, in the mild climate of Sonoma County, California, I grow all the Mediterranean herbs plus mints, borage, summer savory, horseradish, and more. Putting supper together begins with a perusal of the garden to see which herbs are at their best; the other ingredients come next.

Almost all of the herbs listed in this book will flower, sprinkling your herb garden with pretty blossoms. Mix and match, contrast and compare – you can make dramatic and attractive arrangements in dedicated herb gardens, dot herbs through beds and borders, or simply keep a few pots outside the backdoor. This regenerating storecupboard of flavours will ensure triumphant, tasty meals.

Jeff Cox

A NOTE FROM THE COOK MARIE-PIERRE MOINE

As a cook, herbs are my best friends. Just a handful brightens up my emergency storecupboard concoctions: dried pasta and canned tomatoes cry out for warming, peppery basil; haricot beans and flaked tuna for robust parsley and gentle chives; and rice and frozen peas for scented thyme or sage. Half a clove of crushed garlic will not go amiss in any of these impromptu scenarios either.

When I am preparing a more gourmet, formal meal, herbs are wonderful allies, too. And they have power in numbers, so I love putting together a palette of mixed herbs – a bed of rosemary sprigs and thyme underneath a shoulder of lamb, a generous scattering of dried fennel and mustard seeds over belly of pork, and tarragon and parsley in a buttery pan of fried tomatoes. At the end of cooking, I add a scattering of fresh herbs to give a flourish of visual appeal and palate-tingling top notes.

As an urban dweller, I am unable to have a proper herb garden but every year I manage a couple of pots on the windowsill and have never found the need to buy herbs – in the growing months, at least.

Running a hand through stems of rosemary or pinching off basil leaves lifts the spirits, but don't despair if you cannot have fresh herbs permanently on tap; remember that many freeze well. When freezer space is at a premium, herbs should be a priority – a ginger root, a roll of herb butter, or a coriander ice cube are all well worth their shelf space.

Marie - Pierre Moine

CHOOSE

With a huge variety of herbs available, you need to know what flavours you want, how you can use them, and where and how to grow the plants. Whether in a window box, a pot, or in the garden, there's a herb here for everyone.

PLANTED POTS AND BASKETS

The culinary-themed window boxes show you how to produce a whole storecupboard of flavours in one pot. These are just a guide, and you can mix and match them to suit your needs and personal tastes.

KEY:

FROST HARDINESS
* ❋ Half-hardy
* ❋❋ Frost-hardy
* ❋❋❋ Hardy

GROWING CONDITIONS
* ☼ Prefers sun
* ☀ Prefers partial shade
* ☀ Prefers shade
* ◆ Tolerant of wet soil

DIMENSIONS
↕ Height ↔ Spread

EVERYDAY ESSENTIALS

There are some herbs that you return to time and time again to invigorate your cooking. You can make ordinary everyday meals extraordinary with just a handful of these herbs: perk up a roast chicken with sage, add depth to a tomato salad with basil leaves, enliven pasta sauce with oregano, or make a salsa with coriander leaves. And, of course, no cook should be without a fresh supply of thyme and parsley.

SAGE
Salvia officinalis
The evergreen leaves look good year-round in a container. Pick it regularly to encourage the fresh, young leaves that have the finest taste.

CORIANDER
Coriandrum sativum
Many of the most aromatic cuisines, particularly Indian and Asian, value this herb. It prefers semi-shade, so putting it on a sheltered window ledge is ideal.

GROW Most of these herbs grow best in a 50-50 mix of compost and sand to create a well-drained soil. All can withstand some drought except coriander and basil, so water regularly and add an occasional feed of liquid fertilizer in summer.

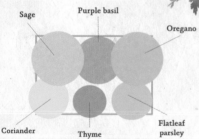

Sage
Purple basil
Oregano
Coriander
Thyme
Flatleaf parsley

HARVEST Pick sage leaves here and there to keep the plant's shape, but cut stems from the other herbs as needed.

PURPLE BASIL
Ocimum basilicum var. ***purpurascens***
This variety is as attractive as it is flavoursome
and really brightens up a container. However,
it needs to be re-planted each year.

OREGANO
Origanum vulgare
This herb thrives in containers, and will keep its
neat shape with a trim after flowering. Cut back
to within 5cm (2in) of the soil in winter.

FLATLEAF PARSLEY
Petroselinum crispum var.
neapolitanum
Flatleaf parsley is an excellent
garnish for soups, stews, and
cooked meats and fish. Pick
leaves regularly to prevent
it growing too big.

THYME
Thymus x *citriodorus*
'Silver Queen'
The pretty variegated
leaves have a strong lemon
scent which, unlike many
herbs, does not disappear
when cooked. Position
in full sun in summer
and away from cold
winds in winter.

Terracotta boxes These look
sensational, but are pervious. The
moisture they absorb, combined with
changing temperatures, often causes
cracks. Choose frost-proof pots or coat
the inside with sealant to protect them.

SALAD HERBS

Each of these herbs has a distinctive flavour, so they should be used in salads in small amounts – except chervil, where more is better. They will happily grow side by side, and can also be used together in recipes, except dill, whose warm caraway-like flavour tends to dominate. Tarragon is a perennial, but the others are annuals or biennials and so will need replacing every year or two.

DILL
Anethum graveolens
Put in its final position when planting this box, as dill doesn't like to be moved. It pairs well with seafood, making an excellent marinade.

ROCKET
Eruca vesicaria subsp. *sativa*
The young leaves have a mild, peppery, pungent flavour, which becomes more pronounced with age. Pick leaves regularly to encourage fresh growth.

GROW These herbs prefer a rich, well-drained, moist (but not wet) soil. Use a 50–50 mix of good garden soil and compost and water regularly, particularly in hot temperatures.

Dill   French tarragon   Chives

Rocket   Curly parsley   Chervil

Pinch off the tips of the herbs to get leaves with full flavour, but allow dill to flower if you are growing it for its seeds.

HARVEST Pick the outer individual leaves of rocket but the whole stems of the others.

FRENCH TARRAGON
Artemisia dracunculus **French**
Plant French not Russian tarragon if you want the anise flavour. Use young plants or grow from cuttings. It is a strong-flavoured herb, so use it sparingly.

CHIVES
Allium schoenoprasum
Chives add a delicate onion aroma and flavour to salads and salsas. Cut individual stems 2.5cm (1in) above soil level and use snipped into small pieces.

CHERVIL
Anthriscus cerefolium
The sweetest herb, in all respects. Chervil's dainty leaves have a light anise and parsley flavour. Plant it in a semi-shady position if you can, as sun causes it to flower too quickly.

CURLY PARSLEY
Petroselinum crispum
This neat herb is perfect for growing in containers; it looks pretty and will not take over the space. Chop the leaves finely and sprinkle over salads.

Wooden trug Drill holes in the base of the trug to allow excess moisture to drain away. Line the trug with black plastic before adding soil, to preserve the wood, and puncture holes in the lining to correspond with those in the base.

MEDITERRANEAN POTS

These herbs are native to the Mediterranean regions. They thrive in free-draining soil and produce the greatest abundance of fragrant, volatile oils when positioned in full sun in hot, dry summers. Mediterranean cuisine is famed for its fresh tastes, and much of that reputation comes from these herbs.

SWEET BASIL
Ocimum basilicum 'Genovese'
Being an annual Mediterranean herb, basil needs sowing under cover each spring, or can be grown indoors on a sunny windowsill.

THYME
Thymus vulgaris
The most well-known variety of this evergreen perennial; it is used in poultry, pork, and fish dishes and in bouquets garnis (see p128).

ROSEMARY
Rosmarinus officinalis
This evergreen perennial form has a strong, piney scent and flavour. It needs regular trimming to keep it in check.

GROW Use free-draining soil, add extra grit to compost if necessary. Plant herbs mixing textures and colours and ensure the pots have some winter use by planting a perennial with each annual.

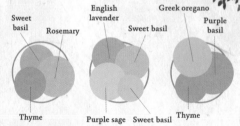

Sweet basil

Rosemary

English lavender

Sweet basil

Greek oregano

Purple basil

Thyme

Purple sage   Sweet basil

Thyme

Water if the leaves droop. Pinch out the tips of the basil and oregano for more leafy growth.

HARVEST Pick basil leaves individually, trim sage leaves here and there to maintain shape.

ENGLISH LAVENDER
Lavandula angustifolia
Use the flowers and evergreen
leaves of this perennial
sparingly in syrups and sugars.

PURPLE SAGE
Salvia officinalis
'Purpurascens'
The leaves of this
evergreen perennial
can be picked all year.

SWEET BASIL
Ocimum basilicum
'Green Ruffles'
and 'Napolitano'
These annual basils have
a spicy aniseed taste.

GREEK OREGANO
Origanum vulgare subsp. *hirtum* 'Greek'
This hardy perennial species has dark,
aromatic leaves. It is popular in
Greek and Turkish dishes.

PURPLE BASIL
Ocimum basilicum var. *purpurascens*
This variety has strongly scented
and richly colourful leaves.

Terracotta pots These
develop a fine patina
over time. The whitish
salt build-up adds
character to them.

MIDDLE EASTERN

Classic dishes from Turkey to Morocco owe their rich, deep flavours to the herb-garden favourites that feature in this zinc container. Traditionally these dishes are accompanied by hot mint tea, which is why this blend of herbs also contains spearmint and another favourite for tea, anise hyssop.

CORIANDER
Coriandrum sativum
As a warmth-loving herb, coriander thrives in pots that can be moved to sunny spots. Trim regularly to encourage leaves, or leave it alone if you want seeds.

GROW All these herbs like well-drained, good-quality potting compost, so add extra grit if necessary. Let coriander flower if you want its seeds. Pinch the growing tip of anise hyssop when young for tender leafy shoots. Water when the soil begins to dry out.

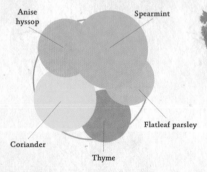

Anise hyssop

Spearmint

Coriander

Flatleaf parsley

Thyme

HARVEST Select individual stems or side branches, or take leaves from here and there.

ANISE HYSSOP
Agastache foeniculum
This herb has a distinct anise flavour in its pretty leaves. It needs protection in hard frosts.

SPEARMINT
Mentha spicata
Spearmint is the most widely grown of all mints. It makes refreshing teas and, in the Middle East, is a key ingredient in tabbouleh (see p152).

FLATLEAF PARSLEY
Petroselinum crispum
var. *neapolitanum*
To ensure a constant supply, sow seed in pots at regular intervals from spring and transfer to the main pot as necessary.

THYME
Thymus vulgaris
The piney, resinous aroma and flavour of thyme is an essential ingredient in Middle Eastern cooking. It is used in lamb tagines and many other dishes.

Zinc container Make a few holes to let excess water drain out and put stones in the base of the pot to aid drainage. Only the mint can tolerate wet roots.

HARDY HERBS

With the exception of rosemary, which needs a winter mulch in some areas, these herbs will survive temperatures down to -29°C (-20°F) and return in spring. Be sure to provide enough room for their roots, as they can grow for years.

GREEK OREGANO
Origanum vulgare subsp. *hirtum* 'Greek'
A more intense version of common oregano, with round, dark green, resinous, peppery leaves.

ORANGE-SCENTED THYME
Thymus x *citriodorus* 'Fragrantissimus'
This variety has evergreen variegated leaves with a distinct citrussy scent. Pick the leaves all year round.

GROW Plant in decent well-drained garden soil with added compost. Remove the top 5cm (2in) of soil in spring and replace with fresh compost.

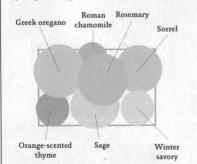

Greek oregano · Roman chamomile · Rosemary · Sorrel · Orange-scented thyme · Sage · Winter savory

HARVEST Cut stems or individual leaves for sorrel and pick chamomile's flowers just as they form buds.

ROMAN CHAMOMILE
Chamaemelum nobile
This is the hardy perennial variety, rather than
the German annual. Use the flower buds in teas,
or let them open to create a pretty feature here.

SORREL
Rumex acetosa
Sorrel is a tangy, sharply acidic, leafy plant.
Remove any flower heads as they appear to
keep fresh, new leaves coming.

ROSEMARY
Rosmarinus officinalis
The resinous quality of this
herb recalls pine and camphor.
It is good with potatoes, lamb,
and in oils.

WINTER SAVORY
Satureja montana
This semi-evergreen
perennial needs winter
protection. Use this potent
herb in small amounts.

SAGE
Salvia officinalis
The leaves can be used in sauces
(see p164), with poultry (see p139),
or in butter for pasta, Italian-style.
They can also be used fresh to make
a soothing tea.

Wooden crate This is roomy enough for these
vigorous herbs, but if they get too big, lift and
divide them when growth is slow, in autumn
or early spring (see p91). Pot on the new extra
plants and return one to the crate.

HERBAL TEAS

The most elegant and flavoursome teas are made using fresh herbs, as the fine fragrance and flavour compounds in their leaves evaporate and disintegrate soon after they're picked. This group includes herbs that can be used to make teas to suit all palates and moods.

LEMON BALM
Melissa officinalis
Use young leaves for a mild lemon-and-mint flavour. Self-sows readily, so root out unwanted seedlings.

BERGAMOT
Monarda didyma
Bergamot makes an excellent herb tea. Dig up plants every three years and divide them.

SWEET WOODRUFF
Galium odoratum
Use sparingly – you need only a stem or two for a mild, vanilla-flavoured tea. Plant under the other herbs, as it likes some shade.

GROW Use potting compost or well-drained garden soil. These plants like moist soil, so tuck dried grass clippings around the base of the stems to conserve moisture. Pinch back the lemon verbena and trim the fennel.

HARVEST Cut just a couple of stems of sweet woodruff and take leaves here and there from the other herbs.

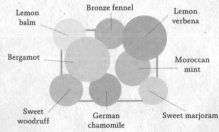

Lemon balm
Bronze fennel
Lemon verbena
Bergamot
Moroccan mint
Sweet woodruff
German chamomile
Sweet marjoram

BRONZE FENNEL
Foeniculum vulgare 'Purpureum'
*With its anise flavour, this fennel makes
a mild tea. Trim the tops for leafy growth.*

LEMON VERBENA
Aloysia triphylla
*With its fragrance and flavour of
lemon but without the acid zing, lemon
verbena is ideal for tea. Cut back stems
once the leaves have dropped.*

MOROCCAN MINT
Mentha spicata var.
crispa 'Moroccan'
*This variety has a fresh
spearmint flavour. It is
widely drunk as a tea in
North Africa. Sink it into
the box in a small pot to
control its growth.*

SWEET MARJORAM
Origanum majorana
*Sweet marjoram is less assertive
than oregano and so makes a
sweet, lightly spicy tea with
a mild camphor note. An annual,
it needs re-sowing each year.*

GERMAN CHAMOMILE
Matricaria recutita
*This annual chamomile is much preferred
for tea over the perennial Roman
chamomile, which has a bitter taste.
Again, it needs re-sowing each year.*

Wicker basket *Weaved wicker gives this
arrangement a rustic feel. Position it in a sunny
spot in summer and move it to a sheltered position
as the plants die back in autumn and winter.*

THE HERB CATALOGUE

What is a herb? A plant needs certain qualities to be a herb; here you will find plants that can quite simply be used to add flavour to your cooking and can be grown in temperate climates. In different cuisines these plants are used in a variety of ways. The leaves, flowers, seeds, or roots are often edible; in some cases leaves and stems are used as "pot herbs", meaning they are boiled and served as a vegetable.

ONION
Allium spp.

These members of the large onion family are useful culinary herbs as well as kitchen staples. They are drought-resistant, and, because they are onions, they rarely have pest problems.

GROW For all these allium species, sweeten good garden soil with wood ash or ground limestone before planting sets or sowing seed, for best results. Ideally, plant garlic in autumn, but you can also plant it in spring along with onions and chives.
HARVEST Dig up bulbils in summer to use or store (see p118) and pick leaves and flowers throughout the growing season as they are needed.
COOK Both garlic and onion bulbils can be used in a wide range of savoury dishes as a flavouring. They keep their flavour well when cooked. Leaves of all the allium species are best used raw.

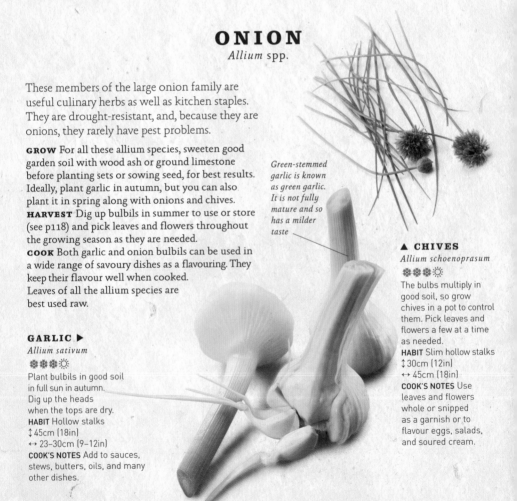

Green-stemmed garlic is known as green garlic. It is not fully mature and so has a milder taste

GARLIC ▶
Allium sativum
✿✿✿☼
Plant bulbils in good soil in full sun in autumn. Dig up the heads when the tops are dry.
HABIT Hollow stalks
↕ 45cm (18in)
↔ 23–30cm (9–12in)
COOK'S NOTES Add to sauces, stews, butters, oils, and many other dishes.

▲ CHIVES
Allium schoenoprasum
✿✿✿☼
The bulbs multiply in good soil, so grow chives in a pot to control them. Pick leaves and flowers a few at a time as needed.
HABIT Slim hollow stalks
↕ 30cm (12in)
↔ 45cm (18in)
COOK'S NOTES Use leaves and flowers whole or snipped as a garnish or to flavour eggs, salads, and soured cream.

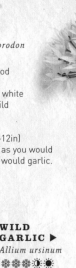

◄ ROCAMBOLE

Allium sativum var. *ophioscorodon*

✻✻✻☼

Plant bulbils in autumn in good
garden soil. Cut the leaves in
spring, dig up the purple and white
bulbils in autumn. It has a mild
garlic flavour.

HABIT Hollow stalks
↕ 45cm (18in) ↔ 23–30cm (9–12in)

COOK'S NOTES Use the leaves as you would
chives and the bulbils as you would garlic.

*The broad
leaves have
a strong
garlicky
aroma*

WILD GARLIC ►

Allium ursinum

✻✻✻☼☼

Sow this perennial
direct into the
garden in moist soil
in semi-shade or
shade in autumn.
Divide established
plants in late
summer. All parts
can be eaten; pick
leaves and flowers
as needed, bulbils in autumn.

HABIT Hollow stalks
↕ 36–45cm (14–18in) ↔ 30cm (12in)

COOK'S NOTES Add leaves and flowers
to salads, or to garnish potato or egg
dishes. Use bulbils in soups, cream
sauces, and in risotto.

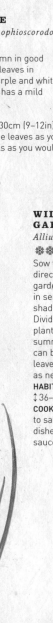

*The leaves of Welsh
onion are round
and hollow*

*Young leaves
have a sweeter
garlic flavour*

GARLIC CHIVES ►

Allium tuberosum

✻✻✻☼

Plant in spring in
good soil. Divide
clumps every three
years. Cut a few
stems as needed.

HABIT Flat-bladed
stalks
↕ 30cm (12in)
↔ 15–20cm (6–8in)

COOK'S NOTES Add to
potato salads.

WELSH ONION ►

Allium fistulosum

✻✻✻☼

Plant sets or sow seed in spring. Divide
clumps every 3 years in spring. Harvest
the oniony bulbs 5–6 weeks after planting.

HABIT Hollow stalks
↕ 20–25cm (8–10in) ↔ 15cm (6in)

COOK'S NOTES Use in egg dishes, quiches,
and savoury tarts.

ANISE HYSSOP
Agastache foeniculum

This relative of mint has minty, anise-flavoured leaves and flowers. It is a perennial, and bees love its pretty purple flower spikes in summer.

✿✿☼☼

GROW Take cuttings or divide plants in spring, or start seed indoors in late winter. Plant out seedlings into good garden soil when all risk of frost has passed. This plant is happiest in full sun and rich, moist soil, but tolerates partial shade.
HARVEST The leaves have the best flavour just before the plant flowers.
COOK Add the leaves and flowers to salads for a mild minty anise flavour, or brew them as a tea.
HABIT Upright, leafy
↕ 60–90cm (24–36in) ↔ 45cm (18in)

The small top leaves make the finest tea

LEMON VERBENA
Aloysia triphylla

The leaves of perennial lemon verbena grow vigorously on long stems, but they keep their lemony scent to themselves until disturbed.

✿✿☼

GROW Plant cuttings in the garden, after all danger of frost has passed, into well-drained, dry soil in full sun. A tender herb, it is best to plant it in a large pot sunk into the ground so it can be moved indoors in autumn in cold regions. In warmer, frost-free areas the plant can stay outside over winter.
HARVEST Leaves can be harvested here and there from the plant and used fresh.
COOK Brew the leaves for citrussy tisanes, use them to make lemony vinegars and oils, or finely chop them and add to salads and fruit desserts.

HABIT Upright, bushy
↕ 3m (10ft) ↔ 3m (10ft)

AMARANTH
Amaranthus hypochondriacus

This annual is a global favourite, with spinach-flavoured leaves and seeds that contain 30 per cent more high-lysine protein than most cereals.

❀ ☀

GROW Sow seed directly into the garden each spring. This herb grows in full sun in almost any kind of soil. Grain amaranth can yield up to 1kg (2.2lb) of grain per plant, so you may need to stake the plants to support their seed heads.

HARVEST Pick leaves as needed, and cut the seed heads with their stems for drying and to collect their seeds (see p116).

COOK Add young leaves to salads and cook mature leaves as you would spinach. Cook seeds in a little water, or in a dry pan to eat as "popcorn".

HABIT Upright, bushy
↕ 1.2–1.5m (4–5ft) ↔ 45–60cm (18–24in)

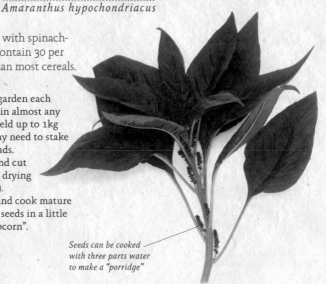

Seeds can be cooked with three parts water to make a "porridge"

DILL
Anethum graveolens

The umbrella-shaped seed heads of this annual bear seeds that are popular for pickling, and the feathery, anise leaves are an excellent flavouring.

❀ ❀ ❀ ☀

GROW Dill is easy to grow from seed; sow in mid-spring in a sunny spot in good, well-drained garden soil where you want it to grow, as it resents disturbance. Position it near plants that will benefit from the insects it attracts. Make successive sowings throughout the summer to keep the crop coming.

HARVEST Use the leaves fresh or dried. Let the seed ripen on the plant before harvesting it (see p106).

COOK Use the seeds in vinegars and teas. Use fresh or dried fronds with salads, and soups; dill goes well with fish, especially salmon, and is a key ingredient in gravlax.

HABIT Upright hollow stems
↕ 60–90cm (24–36in) ↔ 15–30cm (6–12in)

ANGELICA
Angelica archangelica

The leaves and stems of this pretty biennial have an aroma of juniper berries, hence its use in making gin. The seeds and root are edible too.

✿✿✿☼

GROW Sow seed in autumn or spring in semi-shade in a moist, compost-enriched soil where you want it to grow, as its long tap root (the main, largest, vertical root) will not transplant. Water it well in summer, as it dislikes hot, dry conditions. Allow it to set seed in late summer if you want to collect seed or let it self-seed. It will die after setting seed.

HARVEST Take leaves here and there or cut off side shoots before the plant flowers. Collect seeds as they ripen (see p106). Harvest and dry roots in the second autumn just after flowering.

COOK Seeds add a touch of sweetness to drinks; use leaves in custards, marmalades, fruit desserts, and teas; or make candied angelica to decorate cakes.

HABIT Upright, leafy
↕ 30–60cm (12–24in) ↔ 23–30cm (9–12in)

CHERVIL
Anthriscus cerefolium

This annual herb is one of the culinary *fines herbes*, along with chives, parsley, and tarragon. Its lacy leaves have an irresistible, light anise flavour.

✿✿✿☼

GROW Sow seed in moist, compost-enriched soil in a cool, semi-shady spot each spring as temperatures begin to rise. Sow where you want it to grow, as it has a large tap root and dislikes being transplanted. Keep an eye on this plant in summer, as it quickly runs to seed in hot, sunny conditions.

HARVEST Pick leaves from here and there over the plant. Chervil loses flavour when dried, so use the leaves fresh.

COOK The subtle liquorice flavour is fragile, so add the leaves fresh at the last minute to salads and to finish creamy poultry dishes.

HABIT Upright, leafy
↕ 3m (10ft) ↔ 3m (10ft)

SMALLAGE
Apium graveolens

The seeds and leaves of this biennial, wild form of celery have a more intense celery flavour and aroma than the related, large, modern stalks.

❀❀❀◆☀

GROW Sow seed in early spring under cover. Plant out seedlings in full sun in rich compost in the bottom of a shallow trench in the garden, when all risk of frost has passed. Keep the soil well-watered in summer. Let the plant produce its flower heads and set seed if you want to harvest the seeds.

HARVEST Cut individual stalks or the whole plant as and when needed. Harvest the seeds when they are ripe and falling from the seed heads.

COOK Use fresh leaves in salads and sauces, and add the seeds to stews and casseroles.

HABIT Tall, slender stems
↕ 30cm–1m (1–3ft) ↔ 15–30cm (6–12in)

The leaves resemble those of its cousin, parsley

HORSERADISH
Armoracia rusticana

Originally considered a medicinal herb, this perennial is now grown as a culinary herb for its strongly flavoured large tap root and leaves.

❀❀❀☀

GROW Horseradish can be invasive, so plant cuttings or divisions in a large pot sunk into the soil. You need space; the large, wavy-edged leaves spread 60–90cm² (2–3ft²). Choose a sunny spot in sandy, well-drained loam. Enrich with compost in autumn and late spring.

HARVEST Dig up the plant to take pieces of root as needed – the herb is most pungent when freshly dug. Harvest and store all roots in autumn (see p107).

COOK The freshly grated root works wonders mixed with cream to make a sauce, and served with beef or smoked fish.

HABIT Upright, clump-forming
↕ 30cm–1.2m (1–4ft) ↔ 60–90cm (24–36in)

Young leaves can be added to salads

The real flavour is in the root

FRENCH TARRAGON
Artemisia dracunculus French

The flavour of perennial French tarragon is much superior to that of the Russian variety, so cooks prefer to use its anise-flavoured leaves.

❀❀❀☼

GROW This herb doesn't set viable seed, so it must be propagated by root cuttings taken after the first frosts are over (see p90). Plant them out in a warm, dry, sunny spot. Renew old plants by dividing clumps in spring.

HARVEST Pick sprigs of leaves when needed to use fresh. Tarragon freezes well but loses much of its flavour when dried.

COOK Use fresh in omelettes, salads, chicken dishes, and in cream sauces, or to flavour white wine vinegar (see p135).

HABIT Upright, leafy
↕ 45cm–1m (18–36in) ↔ 30–38cm (12–15in)

BORAGE
Borago officinalis

A herb-garden favourite, this annual is cherished more for its sky-blue petals than its leaves, both of which have a cucumber flavour.

❀❀❀☼

GROW Sow seed directly in the garden in mid-spring in well-drained, light soil in a sunny spot. Keep the soil moist during the growing season.

HARVEST Cut young stems for fresh leaves throughout the summer, and pick flowers to use fresh, or to freeze or dry.

COOK Chop the fresh leaves to add to yoghurt, cream, and cucumber salads. Use flowers in drinks such as Pimm's, in ice cubes, salads, or candied to decorate cakes.

HABIT Upright, branching
↕ 30cm–1m (1–3ft) ↔ 15–30cm (6–12in)

The hairs on young leaves dissolve in the mouth on eating

MUSTARDS
Brassica spp.

Grow these annual plants for their peppery leaves and for their seeds, which are used to make the familiar condiment. Black mustard is the most pungent, brown is the bitterest.

✵✵✵☼

GROW Sow seed in autumn in soil enriched with well-rotted manure or compost. The seedlings will emerge in the spring. Alternatively, sow in spring once all risk of frost has passed. Each seed makes a single stem with many flowers, so sow thickly to allow the stems to support one another.
HARVEST Cut the stems with their seed pods just before the seeds ripen and let them dry (see p116). Pick young leaves and flowers all summer.
COOK Add both the leaves and flowers to salads and stir-fry dishes. Crush the seeds for homemade mustard, or add to salad dressings or sauces.

The young seed pods can be pickled

◀ **BROWN MUSTARD**
Brassica juncea
The crinkled-edged leaves have a warm peppery flavour and look pretty in the garden. The seeds are slightly bitter and are less potent than the black ones.
HABIT Upright, clump-forming
↕ 1–1.2m (3–4ft) ↔ 30cm (12in)

The flowers are also edible, with a mild mustard flavour

BLACK MUSTARD ▶
Brassica nigra
Black mustard is harder to find than brown, so it is worth growing your own. The leaves and seeds have a strong flavour and heat.
HABIT Upright, clump-forming
↕ 1–1.2m (3–4ft) ↔ 30cm (12in)

CALAMINT
Calamintha sp.

It is strange that this pretty perennial herb isn't better known for its pleasantly minty, peppery, but slightly bitter leaves and flowers.

✹✹✹☼☀

GROW Start cuttings in pots in early spring, or sow directly into well-drained soil once it has warmed up. Or divide plants in spring. It prefers a slightly alkaline soil, so sweeten acid soil with wood ash or ground limestone. New growth needs protection from severe frosts.

HARVEST Pick leaves when the plant is not in flower for the best flavour. Harvest flowers as and when needed.

COOK Use to flavour drinks, finely chop very young leaves and use in salads. Lesser calamint (*Calamintha nepeta*) has the strongest potency, so use it sparingly.

HABIT Low-growing, bushy
↕ 45cm (18in) ↔ 50–75cm (20–30in)

All parts of the plant have a delicious aroma of mint

POT MARIGOLD
Calendula officinalis

This annual was once known as poor man's saffron because the sweet, edible, yellow or orange flowers are used to dye foods.

✹✹✹☼☀

GROW Sow seed in pots indoors in autumn or in well-drained soil in full sun or partial shade after the last frosts in spring. Transplant into pots or good garden soil in late spring. Marigold is hardy and will overwinter outside in warm climates. The plant produces a small bunch of leaves from which tall daisy-like flowers rise. If growing it in the garden, thin out plants to keep them 30–45cm (12–18in) apart.

HARVEST Pick flowers regularly when they are young and fresh.

COOK You can use the aromatic, slightly bitter petals to decorate salads, or add them to fish and meat stews.

HABIT Bushy, leafy
↕ 50–70cm (20–28in) ↔ 50–70cm (20–28in)

Pick the flowers regularly to encourage more blooms

CHILLI PEPPERS
Capsicum spp.

There are hundreds of chilli pepper varieties available, but listed here are a few of the most popular ones. The plants are perennials in the tropics and annuals in temperate zones.

GROW Sow seed in pots and plant out young plants in rich soil in a sunny position when risk of frost has passed. Mulch the plants and keep the mulch moist to recreate the hot, humid conditions they like.

HARVEST Pepper fruits can range from pea-sized to large cylinders or blocky types. Young peppers are green but ripen to red, yellow, orange, chocolate brown, and other colours. Cut the stems of fruits with scissors when harvesting.

COOK Handle them carefully, scrape out the seeds to lessen their heat, or leave them in for a hotter sensation and the inimitable chilli pepper flavour (see p126). They can be used fresh, dried, in flakes, or ground to spice up many recipes.

◀ SERRANO
Capsicum annuum
The green peppers ripen to red and have very hot, pungent seeds.
HABIT Bushy
↕ Varies, mostly 60cm–1.2m (2–4ft)
↔ 50–90cm (20–36in)
COOK'S NOTES Use in sauces.

BIRD PEPPER ▶
Capsicum annuum
These tiny peppers can be red, orange, or green; their size is deceptive, as they are very, very hot.
HABIT Bushy
↕ Varies, mostly 60cm–1.2m (2–4ft)
↔ 50–90cm (20–36in)
COOK'S NOTES Use whole to add heat to curries.

SCOTCH BONNET ▶
Capsicum chinense
These are one of the hottest peppers on earth. They start yellow-green and ripen to orange-red.
HABIT Bushy
↕ Varies, mostly 60cm–1.2m (2–4ft)
↔ 50–90cm (20–36in)
COOK'S NOTES Use to flavour Caribbean sauces.

JALAPEÑO ▶
Capsicum annuum
A commonly used pepper; when green they are medium-hot, and when ripe and red they are less hot and sweeter.
HABIT Bushy
↕ Varies, mostly 60cm–1.2m (2–4ft)
↔ 50–90cm (20–36in)
COOK'S NOTES Pickle or use as a condiment.

Scotch Bonnet's lantern-shaped fruits are very, very hot

CAPER BUSH
Capparis spinosa

Although a tender native of Mediterranean climates, this evergreen shrub will tolerate warm winters elsewhere, and produces tasty buds.

❋❋☼

GROW Sow seed indoors in early spring or take cuttings. Plant out when risk of frost has passed. It needs good drainage and dry soil. Flower buds are borne on new stems each year, so cut back plants each autumn. Plants raised from seed will not flower for four or five years.
HARVEST Pick flower buds for pickling before they open.
COOK Use the salted or pickled buds in oil- or butter-based sauces, and dressings with fish and cold meats.

HABIT Shrubby
↕ 1m (3ft) ↔ 1.5m (5ft)

Caper bush's pretty white flowers are very ornamental

CARAWAY
Carum carvi

The leaves and seeds of this aromatic, parsley-chervil flavoured biennial are often considered spices, but the root can be used as a pot herb.

❋❋❋☼

GROW Sow seed outdoors in mid-spring in good, well-drained soil in full sun. Once established caraway needs no supplementary feeding, but keep it free of competition from weeds.
HARVEST Gather young leaves as and when required. Cut stems for drying when the seed begins to separate easily from the plant. Dig up plants for the roots in the autumn of their second year.
COOK Use young leaves in salads or soups. Add the seeds to cakes, breads, biscuits, cabbage, cheese dishes, and meat stews.

HABIT Upright, bushy
↕ 1m (3ft) ↔ 30–38cm (12–15in)

Young leaves are less pungent than the seeds

CHAMOMILE
Chamaemelum nobile and *Matricaria recutita*

Perennial Roman chamomile makes a pretty lawn and releases a warm apple scent when walked over. The leaves of annual German chamomile are used to make a soothing tea.

GROW Sow seeds of Roman and German chamomiles under cover in spring. Plant out in well-drained, sandy soil in full sun when all risk of frost has passed. For a lawn, plant close together and cut regularly to encourage dense growth.
HARVEST Cut leaves in spring and early summer; pick flowers when fully open, in mid-summer.
COOK Use the flowers and leaves fresh or dried to make tea; the leaves make a milder brew.

The conical centres of the flowers are dried to use in making tea

GERMAN CHAMOMILE ▶
Matricaria recutita
Plant out seedlings of this annual, flowery flavoured chamomile when they have no more than three true leaves, as they then resent transplanting. Self-sows readily.
HABIT Upright, branching leaves
↕ 60–75cm (24–30in) ↔ 60cm (2ft)

▲ROMAN CHAMOMILE
Chamaemelum nobile
The perennial chamomile has sweet, aromatic, evergreen, lacy foliage with tiny daisy-like flowers. Clip the flowers in the first year and weed around the plant often.
HABIT Low-growing, mat-forming
↕ 15–22cm (6–9in)
↔ indefinite

GOOD KING HENRY/FAT HEN

Chenopodium spp.

The leaves of Good King Henry have an anise flavour while those of Fat Hen have a spinach-like taste. Both are very nutritious, being rich in iron, calcium, and vitamins B1 and C.

❊❊☼

GROW Easily grown in spring from seed sown in well-drained freshly dug soil, or from divisions. These plants are tough survivors and take care of themselves. They like full sun and may need water during droughts.

HARVEST Cut young stems to use like asparagus. Pick young leaves as needed, or harvest larger leaves in summer for cooking.

COOK Use both varieties as a pot herb or eat the young leaves raw in salads.

GOOD KING HENRY

Chenopodium bonus-henricus
This perennial herb resents transplanting, but grows like a weed when established, so you will need to control it.
HABIT Upright, leafy
↕ 60–90cm (24–36in) ↔ 30–45cm (12–18in)
COOK'S NOTES It has an assertive flavour, so use its slightly bitter, lemony leaves sparingly either fresh or dried when cooking beans and pulses.

FAT HEN

Chenopodium album
As a fast-growing annual, Fat Hen will sow itself at will. Remove seedlings if you want to keep it under control.
HABIT Upright, leafy
↕ 30cm–1.8m (1–6ft)
↔ 45–60cm (18–24in)
COOK'S NOTES Use the leaves in mixed green vegetable dishes or in soups; chop finely to add sparingly to salads.

Wash leaves carefully to remove any grit

The leaves are shaped like the imprint of a goose foot

CHICORY
Cichorium intybus

There are many types of this herb, and their leaves, stems, and flowers are used in cuisines around the world.

✿✿✿☼

GROW Sow seed directly into the garden in mid-spring. Cultivated varieties like rich, deep, and well-drained soil to make large tap roots. Give the plants a mid-summer dressing of rich compost. Keep the soil moist but not wet.

HARVEST Cut leaves for salads when very young to use fresh, as older plants develop a bitter, milky sap. Pick flowers in early summer to use fresh or to dry. Dig up roots throughout the summer, or in autumn.

COOK Add young leaves and flowers to salads; lift young roots and boil and serve with a white sauce.

The bitter taste of the leaves mellows when grilled or roasted

RADICCHIO ▶
Cichorium intybus
Cut the bitter, colourful leaves of this annual here and there in mid-summer, then let the plant grow on undisturbed to produce tight heads for autumn.
HABIT Upright, tight head of leaves
↕ 15–20cm (6–8in) ↔ 20–25cm (8–10in)
COOK'S NOTES Add the leaves to salads, chargrill with olive oil, or roast, or stew.

BELGIAN ENDIVE ▶
Cichorium intybus
Keep the tall leaves of this perennial pale for a less bitter flavour. Pot up the plants in early winter and put them in a dark place indoors for 4–6 weeks to "force" chicons, which are blanched stems.
HABIT Upright, tight head of leaves
↕ 60cm (24in) ↔ 30cm (12in)
COOK'S NOTES Use leaves in winter salads with walnuts and a creamy dressing, sprinkle chicons with lemon juice and steam, or bake with cheese and ham.

▲LOOSELEAF CHICORY
Cichorium intybus 'Roseum'
Sow seed of this mild-tasting annual in spring for a winter crop. This variety has pink flowers, but usually they are blue.
HABIT Upright
↕ 45–60cm (18–24in) ↔ 20–25cm (8–10in)
COOK'S NOTES Dry roots, then roast and grind them to use as a substitute for coffee; young leaves make a good salad.

BALM OF GILEAD
Cedronella canariensis

This perennial is usually grown as an annual.
It has a musky scent that is used in potpourris.
The bitter leaves can be brewed for tea.

❋ ☼

GROW Sow seed under cover in a sunny spot and
plant out when all danger of frost is past. It needs
good drainage but plenty of moisture during the
growing season. The plant flowers late in the season.
HARVEST Pick leaves before the plant flowers for
the best flavour; they can be used fresh or dried.
COOK Add the leaves to tea blends.

HABIT Upright, shrubby
↕ 1.5m (5ft) ↔ 1m (3ft)

*The leaves
have a strong
eucalyptus scent*

EDIBLE CHRYSANTHEMUM
Chrysanthemum coronarium

The bitter leaves and flowers of this annual are
widely used as a flavouring in cooking in Asia,
especially in China and Japan.

❋ ❋ ❋ ☼

GROW Sow seed in spring, in moist soil in full sun.
Water frequently.
HARVEST Take leaves here and there all summer.
Pick flowers as they appear to use fresh, let some
flowers dry on the stem and crumble them to store.
COOK Add petals to salads, or blanch flower
heads for one minute and serve with a savoury
sauce. Use young leaves and stems in stir-fries,
stews, and soups.

HABIT Upright, branching
↕ 90cm (36in) ↔ 40cm (16in)

*Petals, or the
entire flower
head, can be
used in cooking*

CORIANDER
Coriandrum sativum

The leaves of this annual herb have a slightly pungent citrussy flavour, while the seeds have a sweet, warm, woody fragrance.

✤✤✤☼

GROW Sow seed in rich, moist soil in a protected sunny spot. If you want seeds as well as leaves, do not deadhead the flowers, and leave the seeds to ripen from green to light brown in colour.

HARVEST Pick leaves all summer. Pick seed heads and dry fully before storing the seeds.

COOK Use fresh chopped leaves in salads, with coconut, citrus, avocado, fish, and meat. The dried seeds are spicy, sweet, and mildly orange-flavoured – use them in curries and oriental dishes.

HABIT Upright, bushy
↕ 15–70cm (6–28in) ↔ 10–30cm (4–12in)

Coriander leaves look similar to those of flatleaf parsley

CUMIN
Cuminum cyminum

An ancient annual herb, today it is grown and used worldwide. The seeds of this delicate plant have a rich earthy flavour, so use them sparingly.

✤☼

GROW Sow seed in good, moist soil in full sun. Keep the plants well watered as drought can prevent them setting seed. Cumin is a floppy, thin-stemmed plant that grows best when draped over a support frame of chicken wire.

HARVEST Pick leaves as needed. When the plant browns and the seeds are dry, cut the stems and hang them to dry completely. Collect the seeds as they are released (see p116).

COOK Use the leaves in salads and spicy dishes. Once ground, dried seeds are pungent, sharp, and indispensable in Middle Eastern and oriental dishes. Cumin is often used with coriander and chickpeas.

HABIT Slender, upright
↕ 15–30cm (6–12in) ↔ 8–10cm (3–4in)

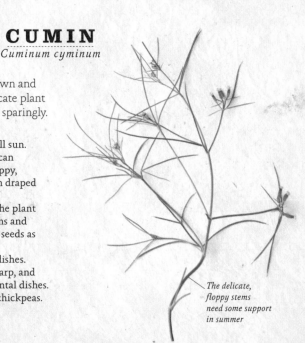

The delicate, floppy stems need some support in summer

CITRUS
Citrus spp.

Even in cold areas you can have a taste of the Mediterranean. These four perennial citrus plants will thrive on the patio in summer and indoors in winter. Their zest and juices add a tart flavour to both sweet and savoury dishes.

❀☀

GROW Plant woody shrubs or trees in generous pots of rich, sandy, well-drained soil that can be moved to a bright place indoors when the freezing weather arrives. Buy young plants at the nursery that are on dwarfing rootstock. Keep them in full sun and water regularly, but give them a steady supply of nitrogen by watering with liquid fertilizer. Root prune and re-pot them after 4–5 years.
HARVEST Citrus fruits store well on the tree; pick as needed.
COOK Use dried peel to flavour stews, puddings, and sweet sauces. Add candied peel to cakes.

ORANGE ▲
Citrus sinensis
The flowers and, of course, the fruits have a strong orange aroma. Some varieties can be tart or bitter. Navel oranges have the best flavour; they are seedless with a navel-like formation at one end.
HABIT Upright tree
↕ 4.5–6.1m (15–20ft) ↔ 3.6–4.5m (12–15ft)
COOK'S NOTES Use flowers in teas and tisanes, and the zest and juice of the fruit in stews, with duck, and in puddings.

KUMQUAT ▶
Fortunella japonica
This compact plant produces small, slightly bitter, oval, orange fruits. Plant the superior-flavoured variety *Fortunella crassifolia* 'Meiwa' if you can find it.
HABIT Medium-sized, bushy shrub
↕ 1.8–4.5m (6–15ft)
↔ 3–3.6m (10–12ft)
COOK'S NOTES Stew the yellow to red-orange fruits in Middle Eastern savoury dishes, such as tagines.

The fruits produce an aromatic rind as well as juice and flesh that can be used in sweet and savoury dishes

LIME ▶
Citrus aurantiifolia

This small tree produces round green fruits with a pleasantly sour taste in late summer. Bearss lime (*Citrus x latifolia*) is a good variety. The leaves of the kaffir lime (*Citrus hystrix*) are used in Thai cooking.

HABIT Open structure
↕ 3–5m (10–15ft)
↔ 2–3m (6–10ft)

COOK'S NOTES Limes go well with herbs and spices such as ginger, coriander, parsley, dill, and fenugreek. Add to chicken, fish, and lamb dishes.

Fruits have a zingy zest but slightly sour, sharp flesh

LEMON ▶
Citrus limon

These are popular pot plants, which bear white, highly scented flowers and yellow, sharp fruits. A reliable, easy-to-grow and compact variety is 'Meyer Lemon', which will flower all year.

HABIT Medium-sized shrub
↕ 1.2–1.8m (4–6ft) in a generous pot
↔ 1.2–1.5m (4–5ft)

COOK'S NOTES The sharp juice is good in salad dressings and puddings. The fruit can be used fresh or preserved, whole with roast poultry, in vegetable dishes, tagines, or sliced with fish or grilled meats and poultry.

Preserve whole lemons in salt and use the rind in stews and tagines

LEMONGRASS
Cymbopogon citratus

This tropical, evergreen, perennial grass contains the same volatile oil as lemon rind, and so the stems impart a fresh, clean, citrussy flavour.

❁ ☼

GROW Sow seed in pots indoors in spring or divide established plants. Plant young plants outdoors in a sunny spot in good, moist soil. In temperate climates, grow in a generous pot. Lemongrass copes well outdoors during the summer, but take it indoors for the cold months.
HARVEST Cut the fresh leaves and lower stems of single stalks as needed.
COOK Fresh stems and leaves add a distinctive flavour to Thai curries and South East Asian dishes, such as salads, spring rolls, and fish dishes.

HABIT Clump-forming, with cane-like stems
↕ 1.2m (4ft) ↔ 1m (3ft)

The stems and bases can be stored, whole, in a plastic bag in the fridge or frozen

MEADOWSWEET
Filipendula ulmaria

Dense panicles of fragrant white flowers earn this perennial herb a place in ornamental gardens. The flowers and leaves are cucumber flavoured.

❁❁❁💧☼

GROW Sow seed indoors in late winter for setting out in mid-spring, or divide established plants in autumn. Meadowsweet is a marsh plant that needs a constantly wet, neutral to slightly alkaline soil and semi-shade. Avoid the cultivar 'Plena', as it is prone to mildew.
HARVEST You can pick flowers throughout the summer but take the leaves in mid-summer only.
COOK Traditionally used to make beer, the fresh flowers and crushed leaves also add a delicate, mild flavour to jams, stews, and drinks.

HABIT Clump-forming
↕ 60cm–1.2m (2–4ft) ↔ 45cm (18in)

Pick flowers just as they open and use fresh or dry

ROCKET

Eruca vesicaria subsp. *sativa*

The rocket family includes many different varieties; most are edible herbs, but some are preferred for fragrance. Here are a few good culinary types.

❀ ❀ ☼ ☀

GROW Sow seed in early spring in pots or directly in well-drained soil. Water well during the growing season. Rocket runs to seed quickly; don't let plants flower unless you want them to self-seed. Be warned, slugs and snails also love to eat the leaves.

HARVEST The leaves are ready before the hot weather arrives. Pick a few at a time, and leave the others to grow on.

COOK Add raw, whole leaves to salads. Use the leaves when young, as they become bitter with age.

Fragrant flower heads make this a welcome addition to the garden

◀ WILD ROCKET

Diplotaxis muralis

This annual enjoys any good soil. The dandelion-like leaves have a bitter, peppery flavour.

HABIT Upright, leafy
↕ 30–45cm (12–18in)
↔ 25–30cm (10–12in)

COOK'S NOTES Use sparingly in mixed leaf salads, chop and add to soups and cooked dishes, or pair with chickpeas.

SWEET ROCKET ▶

Hesperis matronalis

This biennial herb is grown for its fragrant flower heads, which, like its bitter leaves, are also edible.

HABIT Upright, leafy
↕ 60–90cm (24–36in)
↔ 30–45cm (12–18in)

COOK'S NOTES Use leaves and flowers in salads.

ROCKET ▶

Eruca vesicaria subsp. *sativa*

This annual tolerates dappled shade as well as full sun. Keep soil moist.

HABIT Upright, leafy
↕ 15–25cm (6–10in)
↔ 20–30cm (8–12in)

COOK'S NOTES Use young leaves in salads, or cook as you would spinach.

FENNEL
Foeniculum vulgare

Do not confuse this perennial with Florence fennel, a bulbous-based vegetable. This herb is grown for its anise-flavoured leaves and seeds.

❀ ❀ ❀ ☼

GROW Sow seed in spring. Fennel is happy in most soils as long as it has full sun. It is a tall, aromatic plant, which bears an abundant crop of seeds each year. Water well until established. In autumn, cut the stems to 2.5cm (1in) above the ground; they will return in spring.

HARVEST Cut stalks and leaves in early summer before the stems turn woody. Harvest seed heads for drying when they are yellow-green (see p116).

COOK Use the leaves in marinades for pork, chicken, and lamb, or in salad dressings. Use seeds or fronds with sea bass or oily fish such as salmon.

BRONZE FENNEL ▶
Foeniculum vulgare 'Purpureum'
Pick leaves early in the season, and let new growth ripen over the summer. It is shorter and less vigorous than ordinary fennel, with a milder anise flavour.
HABIT Tall, upright stems
↕ 90cm–1.5m (3–5ft) ↔ 25–30cm (10–12in)
COOK'S NOTES Use seeds and leaves in vinegar, tea, breads, cakes, pies, and sausages. Sprouting seeds are good in salads.

◀ **GREEN FENNEL**
Foeniculum vulgare
Don't plant near dill or they may hybridize. Replant every 3–4 years. A graceful plant with feathery leaves and an anise flavour throughout.
HABIT Tall, upright stems
↕ 1.5–1.8m (5–6ft) ↔ about 30cm (12in)

SWEET WOODRUFF
Galium odoratum

A pretty, perennial groundcover plant with profuse, tiny white flowers. The flowers, stems, and leaves all have a delicate vanilla flavour.

✿✿✿☀

GROW Sow seed in well-drained soil in spring. It prefers semi-shade to full shade, which makes it useful under and around shrubs. It self-sows freely once established.

HARVEST Cut and dry flowers and leaves together in early summer.

COOK Traditionally used to prepare punches and wine cups, such as May wine in Germany, and in cocktails. Sprinkle tiny flowers on salads, but use sparingly. Brew a calming tea with young leaves.

HABIT Creeping
↕ 50cm (20in) ↔ indefinite

The aroma of the plant is strengthened when it is wilted or dried

HOPS
Humulus lupulus

The male flowers grow in yellowish clusters and can be cooked

Hops are well-known for flavouring beer, and the female flowers of this perennial vine are also used to make tea. The stems can be steamed.

✿✿✿☀

GROW Plant young plants in rich soil in full sun. With regular water, the common hop will cover a massive amount of aerial space. Because it grows so fast, you need to enrich deep soil with plenty of compost to nourish it. It will need a large arbour, extensive trellis, or an open tree to grow into.

HARVEST Pick young, fresh side shoots in spring. Collect the female flowers – tiered flaky bracts with tiny flowers between them – while fresh and green, and the male flowers as needed.

COOK Blanch young shoots and serve hot as spring greens, or use in soups or salads. Parboil male flowers and add to salads when cold.

HABIT Climbing
↕ 3–6m (10–20ft) ↔ indefinite

HYSSOP
Hyssopus officinalis

The leaves and flowers of this perennial herb
have a strong, minty, slightly bitter flavour.
In mild winter areas the leaves are evergreen.

❋❋❋☼

GROW Sow seed indoors in late winter. Transplant
to pots by early spring, and set out in a sunny spot
in the garden by mid-spring. Hyssop tolerates dry
soil but does better when watered as needed. Trim
the top shoots to encourage bushy growth.
HARVEST In some areas leaves can be picked year
round. Cut flowers in summer when they are
fully open.
COOK Add the pungent fresh flowers to fruit dishes
and salads sparingly, and use the powerful leaves in
moderation in pies, and meat or game dishes.

HABIT Dwarf shrub
↕ 45–60cm (18–24in) ↔ 90cm (3ft)

*The leaves release
their aroma when
brushed against,
which makes it a good
plant for hedging*

JASMINE
Jasminum officinale

This perennial climber emits one of the most
exotic perfumes in the world, and its highly
scented flowers can be used in cooking.

❋❋❋☼◑

GROW Buy young vines at the nursery and plant
them in well-drained soil against a wall, fence, or
trellis. Jasmine can withstand temperatures down
to -1°C (30°F). The vine blooms best with full
sun, regular watering, and rich soil, but
tolerates some shade.
HARVEST Pick the blossoms just before
they open, from summer until early autumn.
COOK Use the flowers fresh in infusion for tea,
and occasionally desserts.

HABIT Climbing
↕ 10m (30ft) ↔ indefinite

*Pick flowers
while still buds*

JUNIPER
Juniperus communis

Often found in borders, these perennial shrubs have prickly evergreen leaves and bear their edible piney-flavoured berries year round.

❀❀❀☼◑☀

GROW Sow seed or grow from cuttings in spring or autumn, or buy a plant of modest size. Juniper grows in any well-drained soil. Position in full sun in cold regions, or partial shade where summers are hot. They need no fertilizing, but water occasionally in dry summers. They do not like boggy soil.

HARVEST Pick berries when they are dark, almost black, with a bluish bloom in late summer.

COOK Berries traditionally flavour gin and other spirits. To enjoy their flavour in food, crush them and use in marinades, meat stews, pot roasts, stuffings, and winter cabbage dishes. Use fresh, dried, or frozen.

HABIT Upright, spreading or prostrate shrub
↕ 2–4m (6–12ft) ↔ 2–4m (6–12ft)

Harvest the berries when they are almost black

BAY
Laurus nobilis

The ancients crowned victors with wreaths of bay leaves; today cooks have many uses for them. This evergreen shrub bears bitter leaves all year.

❀❀☼

GROW Sow seed in spring or buy young plants. In cooler regions, plant in a generous pot that can be moved indoors during the winter. If planting in the garden it will tolerate any soil as long as it is well drained and in full sun. The plant will withstand summer droughts. Prune it back if you want to create a smaller shrub.

HARVEST Pick dark green, leathery leaves any time.

COOK Mix with thyme and parsley to make a bouquet garni; allow to dry a little or use frozen leaves in meat stews, poultry and fish dishes, and custards. Do not store beyond 3–4 months or the leaves lose their aroma.

HABIT Dense tree
↕ 3–15m (10–50ft) ↔ 10m (30ft)

Fresh leaves have a stronger flavour than dried ones

LAVENDER
Lavandula spp.

The sweetly camphorous scent of this perennial defines freshness. The flowers have the strongest scent, but you can also use the leaves in cooking.

GROW These are good drought-tolerant plants once established, so plant young plants or cuttings in poor, sandy, dry soils in full sun where they will produce more of their aromatic oils. Deadhead spent flowers in late summer and cut back the plant to within a few centimetres of the older stems in autumn (see p96). Do not cut into the woody part of the stem or it will kill the plant.

HARVEST Pick flower heads and cut stems when the flowers first open. Harvest leaves at any time.

COOK Use in moderation. Flowers add flavour to desserts, ice cream, sugar, biscuits such as shortbread, and drinks. Leaves make a good alternative to rosemary in stews and stuffings.

Tall, fragrant flower heads rise above bushy growth

Violet bracts appear almost year round in warmer climates

◄ FRENCH LAVENDER
Lavandula dentata
❋☼
The short, grey-green, aromatic, evergreen leaves have a more pungent, camphor note than English lavender.
HABIT Upright shrub
↕ 30–60cm (12–24in)
↔ 30–45cm (12–18in)

Short evergreen leaves have a pungent note

ENGLISH LAVENDER ▲
Lavandula angustifolia
❋❋❋☼
The most aromatic of the lavenders, with a milder, more floral scent than the intense Mediterranean lavenders. Don't fertilize and don't overwater.
HABIT Upright shrub
↕ 30–60cm (12–24in)
↔ 30–45cm (12–18in)

LOVAGE
Levisticum officinale

This perennial herb has a sharp, penetrating, celery-like flavour throughout its seeds, stalks, and leaves, so only cook with small quantities.

❀❀❀☼◐

GROW Sow seed indoors in late winter. Set out started plants in good garden soil in a protected spot once all risk of frost has passed. They will need adequate water and protection from full sun in the hottest regions. Divide plants in spring or autumn.
HARVEST Pick leaves and stalks in summer. Harvest seed heads by cutting down stems when the seeds start to turn brown, then dry (see p116).
COOK Young shoots can be eaten raw or blanched as a spring vegetable. Add chopped leaves to salads, soups, stews, and stocks for a strong, aromatic, celery flavour.

HABIT Low-growing mound with tall stems
↕ 2m (6ft) ↔ 1m (3ft)

Use lovage seed in cooking as you would celery seed

LEMON BALM
Melissa officinalis

The highly aromatic leaves of this perennial give the impression of lemon with a hint of mint. The flowers are also much loved by bees.

❀❀❀☼◐

GROW Divide plants in autumn or spring, or sow seed in spring in any good soil in a sunny spot; in very hot regions it will need some shade. Lemon balm self-sows with abandon and will be a pest if not controlled.
HARVEST Pick young leaves throughout the summer and use them fresh, because the flavour is delicate and fades as the leaves age and when dried.
COOK Use fresh baby leaves to add a delicate lemon-mint flavour to tea, and fruit and wine drinks. Chop and mix with soft cheeses.

HABIT Upright, bushy
↕ 60cm (24in) ↔ 45cm (18in)

The leaves look like mint, but release a citrussy scent when crushed

BERGAMOT
Monarda didyma

This pretty perennial has a place in both the ornamental and herb garden. The aromatic leaves and flowers both have culinary uses.

❀❀❀💧☼☀

GROW Sow seed indoors in late winter or directly in the garden from early spring to mid-summer, or grow from cuttings in early summer. It likes good, well-drained garden soil and full sun to dappled shade. Its volatile oils make it resistant to insect damage. Divide plants in early spring (see p91).
HARVEST The hot, high summer days are the best time to pick leaves and flowers.
COOK Use fresh leaves when brewing tea or add them to stuffings for pork and poultry. Scatter the flower petals over salads.

HABIT Upright, bushy
↕ 90cm–1.2m (3–4ft) ↔ 30–60cm (12–24in)

CURRY LEAF
Murraya koenigii

This small, perennial tree can only be grown outdoors in the tropics, but you can grow it indoors elsewhere for its musky, citrussy leaves.

❀☼

GROW In tropical climates, sow seed directly into rich garden soil or grow from semi-ripe cuttings in late spring or early summer. Elsewhere, sow in pots in a hot, sunny spot indoors. Water well, as it is a thirsty plant.
HARVEST Fresh leaves are available most of the year, except for during a short winter spell. They freeze well in freezer bags.
COOK Use fresh, dried, or from frozen in vegetarian curries, with pork, or in stuffings for samosas.

HABIT Tall shrub or small tree
↕ 6m (20ft) ↔ 3–5m (10–15ft)

SWEET CICELY
Myrrhis odorata

The ferny foliage and white flowers of this hardy perennial carry a light anise scent, leading some to call it Great Chervil. All parts are edible.

✿ ✿ ✿ ☀

GROW Sow seed in autumn directly in the garden, or grow from root cuttings in spring or autumn. This plant prefers light shade and humusy soil, as you would find in the woods. Best for the shady part of the herb garden; if planted in sun, its leaves yellow and die in summer, returning in autumn.

HARVEST Stalks, stems, and leaves can all be harvested at any time. Collect fresh seeds when they are green, ripe seeds to dry when dark brown.

COOK Stew leaves with fruit to reduce tartness, or add to salads and egg dishes. Use fresh seeds in ice cream and fruit salads, dried seeds in puddings, and grate the root or cook as a vegetable.

HABIT Large, open
↕ 1–2m (3–6ft) ↔ 60cm–1.2m (2–4ft)

The fern-like leaves smell of anise when crushed

MYRTLE
Myrtus communis

The leaves and flower buds of this perennial shrub are spicy with fragrant flowers. Like juniper, the seeds can be ground as a spice.

✿ ✿ ☀

GROW Take softwood cuttings in spring and semi-hardwood ones in summer and grow on in pots or out in the garden. It prefers well-drained soil of medium fertility in full sun. Myrtle needs little care and can withstand summer droughts.

HARVEST Pick leaves, unopened flower buds, open flowers, and berries as they appear in summer.

COOK Add the flower buds to salads (without the green parts) and use the berries for their gently resinous orange-blossom flavour. Dry and grind the berries in a pestle and mortar before using.

HABIT Dense, mounded shrub
↕ 1.5–1.8m (5–6ft) ↔ 1.2–1.5m (4–5ft)

MINT

Mentha spp.

This perennial herb is grown everywhere and is used to flavour just about anything. Spearmint and peppermint are the two most popular kinds, but there are many others.

✤✤✤💧☀

GROW Sow seed in spring, or take root cuttings or divide clumps. Mint likes rich, wet soil, full sun, or dappled shade in hot regions. Mint spreads rapidly by underground rhizomes, so keep plants in check by planting them in pots.
HARVEST Pick leaves or whole stems when young and fresh.
COOK Mints have a dominant flavour, so use sparingly with other herbs to enhance delicate ingredients. The flavoured varieties have subtle aromas, which evaporate quickly: add them to lamb, dairy, and vegetable dishes, and fruit and chocolate desserts at the last minute.

MOROCCAN MINT ▶

Mentha spicata var. *crispa* 'Moroccan'
Best grown away from other mints, as this mint hybridizes easily. It has a clean, slightly spicy, mint flavour.
HABIT Upright, bushy
↕ 30–45cm (12–18in) ↔ 60–90cm (24–36in)
COOK'S NOTES Use in all dishes needing mint, and for brewing tea.

Mint family members have square stems

SPEARMINT ▶

Mentha spicata
Has a clean flavour but loses potency after flowering. Cut back to 15–20cm (6–8in) to promote new growth. Divide clumps.
HABIT Upright, spreading
↕ 25–45cm (10–18in) or more
↔ 60–90cm (24–36in) or more
COOK'S NOTES Serve very fresh sprigs with tarragon with barbecued meats.

Stems and leaf veins are reddish-purple when grown in good, moist soil

◀ CHOCOLATE MINT
Mentha x *piperita citrata* 'Chocolate'
The dark green to purple leaves have a distinct chocolate-mint smell.
HABIT Upright, bushy
↕ 30–45cm (12–18in) ↔ 60–90cm (24–36in)
COOK'S NOTES Add to ice creams, chocolate puddings, and berries. Particularly good with raspberries.

APPLE MINT ▶
Mentha suaveolens
A vigorous plant with downy leaves that have a slight apple aroma.
HABIT Spreading
↕ 45–60cm (18–24in)
↔ 60–90cm (24–36in) or more
COOK'S NOTES Good for flavouring cider vinegar, and adding to sauces.

GINGER MINT ▲
Mentha x *gracilis (syn. M* x *gentilis)*
A hardy perennial with a delicate, warm flavour.
HABIT Spreading
↕ 45–60cm (18–24in)
↔ 60–90cm (24–36in) or more

Slightly hairy leaves have a strong peppermint scent

◀ BLACK PEPPERMINT
Mentha x *piperita* var. *piperita*
'Black Peppermint'
This is a choice variety with dark purple stems and dark green, oval, strongly peppermint-scented leaves.
HABIT Spreading
↕ 45–60cm (18–24in)
↔ 60–90cm (24–36in) or more
COOK'S NOTES Use sparingly in desserts, or in teas.

PEPPERMINT ▶
Mentha x *piperita*
A tall-growing hybrid with a strong minty flavour.
HABIT Spreading
↕ 60cm (24in) ↔ 90cm (36in) or more

CRESSES
Nasturtium

The cresses listed here are not aromatic but have a pleasant, crisp, peppery flavour in their leaves and their succulent stems.

GROW Sow seed in pots or in garden soil in early spring. Both varieties like a sunny spot.
HARVEST Cut the leaves as required.
COOK The leaves of both cresses give a peppery flavour to salads and make a good garnish.

GARDEN CRESS ▶
Lepidium sativum
✸✸✸☼
This annual herb grows from seed to very spicy, peppery cress in just a week in ordinary garden soil and is ready to harvest a few weeks later. Often planted with mustard seed to produce lively micro-greens.
HABIT Low growing
↕ 7.5cm (3in) ↔ indefinite
COOK'S NOTES Use in sandwiches and as a peppery finish to dishes and salads.

WATERCRESS ▶
Nasturtium officinale
✸✸✸💧☼
Sow seed in alkaline soil. It will grow in pots or the garden if the soil is kept constantly wet. Pick the stems in late spring/early summer.
HABIT Low-growing, sprawling
20–25cm (8–10in) indefinite
COOK'S NOTES Wilt florets in pan juices and serve them with meat; or use in soups and savoury tarts.

PERILLA
Perilla spp.

This annual herb is better known as shiso in Japan and much of Asia. The decorative leaves of both types have a spicy scent that is reminiscent of cinnamon and cloves.

❀ ❀ ☼

GROW This herb must be grown as an annual, as it doesn't withstand frost. Sow seed in spring indoors in pots or outdoors in a sunny spot and well-drained soil once all risk of frost has passed. Give plants a mid-summer drink of liquid fertilizer. Move pots indoors in winter or if frost is forecast.
HARVEST Pick leaves or growing tips here and there at any time.
COOK Add fresh to noodle soups, spring rolls, and fish, rice, and vegetable dishes.

◄ GREEN PERILLA
Perilla frutescens var. *crispa*
The green variety does not like to be waterlogged. Pinch out the growing tips to force more of the leaves. The flavour is more potent than in the red variety.
HABIT Upright, bushy
↕ 60–90cm (24–36in)
↔ 60cm (24in)
COOK'S NOTES It is used as a vegetable in Japanese cuisine.

The pretty, frilly red leaves look good in food and the garden

PURPLE PERILLA ▶
Perilla frutescens var. *purpurascens*
The red variety is not as vigorous as the green one, nor as potent, but it does self-sow readily. Gather seed to sow the next spring.
HABIT Upright, bushy
↕ 60cm (24in) ↔ 30cm (12in)
COOK'S NOTES Use in cake mixes and drinks or as a dye when pickling vegetables.

BASIL

Ocimum basilicum spp.

Basil is one of the must-have annual herbs to grow in or for the kitchen. The cinnamon-anise-mint aroma and flavour of its leaves contributes to many cuisines around the world.

✿✿✿☼

GROW Sow seed in spring and throughout the summer in well-drained soil or pots. It likes full sun and adequate moisture. The plant stops growing leaves and loses flavour when it flowers, so pinch out flower buds as they appear. Give the plant a mid-summer feed of liquid fertilizer.

HARVEST Pick young stems with their shiny leaves as they are needed.

COOK The tomato, of course, is basil's perfect partner. Basil's flavour intensifies when cooked, for a more subtle taste, use it raw or add it at the end of cooking.

SWEET BASIL ▶

Ocimum basilicum

A strongly scented variety with large, bright green leaves.

HABIT Upright, bushy

↕ 60–75cm (2–2½ft) ↔ 60cm (2ft)

COOK'S NOTES Use in pesto, salads, tomato sauces, and soups.

Keep a pot of basil in the kitchen; the scent of the leaves repels flies

GREEK BASIL ▶

Ocimum minimum 'Greek'

This easy-to-grow variety has the smallest leaves of all, but they still have a good flavour.

HABIT Compact, bushy

↕ 15–30cm (6–12in)

↔ 15–30cm (6–12in)

COOK'S NOTES Add whole leaves to salads and tomato sauces.

LEMON BASIL ▶

Ocimum x citriodorum

Both the leaves and flowers of this variety have a fresh, clean, lemony scent.

HABIT Compact, bushy

↕ 45cm (18in)

↔ 30–60cm (12–24in)

COOK'S NOTES It is excellent in tomato salads and fish stews.

◀ PURPLE RUFFLES BASIL

Ocimum basilicum var. *purpurascens* 'Purple Ruffles'

Similar to Purple Basil but this variety has less flavour. It is tricky to raise from seed.

HABIT Upright, bushy
‡ 60–75cm (24–30in)
↔ 60cm (24in)

The large leaves have a ruffled, frilly appearance

THAI BASIL ▶

Ocimum basilicum 'Horapha'

The leaves carry a sweet anise and peppery aroma and a strong anise flavour.

HABIT Sturdy, compact, bushy
‡ 30–45cm (12–18in) ↔ 30cm (12in)
COOK'S NOTES Much-used in Thailand, add sparingly to coconut curries and other spicy dishes.

HOLY BASIL ▲

Ocimum sanctum

The green leaves have a spicy aroma. It originates in Thailand, where it is grown around Buddhist temples.

HABIT Vigorous, upright
‡ 45–60cm (18in–24in) ↔ 60cm (24in)
COOK'S NOTES A staple ingredient in Thai cooking, such as in stir-fries with chicken, beef, or pork.

The leaves release a strong cinnamon scent when bruised

◀ CINNAMON BASIL

Ocimum basilicum 'Cinnamon'

Native to Mexico, this basil has clear cinnamon notes.

HABIT Upright, bushy
‡ 30–60cm (12–24in)
↔ 45cm (18in)
COOK'S NOTES Tear leaves and add to South American dishes, and use in desserts.

PURPLE BASIL ▲

Ocimum basilicum var. *purpurascens*

A striking plant with its dark maroon-purple, almost black leaves. The leaves have a distinct clove and mint flavour.

HABIT Upright, bushy
‡ 60–75cm (2–2½ft) ↔ 60cm (24in)
COOK'S NOTES Use to flavour oils and butter, and as a garnish.

OREGANO AND MARJORAM
Origanum spp.

These herbs are different species in the same genus. Their aromatic leaves are delicious in cooking. Both are perennials, but marjoram is often grown as an annual in cold-winter areas.

GROW Sow seed in pots in early spring or in the garden in mid-spring in full sun. You can increase plants by root division (see p90). Do not enrich the soil or feed the plants; a poor soil forces the plant to produce more of the volatile oils that give the leaves their aroma and flavour.

HARVEST Pick leaves at any time, but they are at their finest just before flowering.

COOK Their pungent, spicy flavour gives a unique lift to Mediterranean ingredients and dishes – pizza, pasta, fish, meat, beans, tomatoes, aubergines, and courgettes.

Greek oregano has dark green leaves that are slightly hairy

OREGANO ▲
Origanum vulgare
✿✿✿☼

The stems often flop when the flower heads mature. Cut back after flowering to prevent straggly growth. Use fresh or frozen for maximum impact. Oregano keeps its peppery flavour well when dried, too.
HABIT Bushy
↕ 60–90cm (24–36in) ↔ 90cm–1.2m (3–4ft)

◀ GREEK OREGANO
Origanum vulgare subsp. *hirtum* 'Greek'
✿✿✿☼

The dark green leaves have a strong, resinous aroma and are excellent for cooking.
HABIT Bushy
↕ 60cm (24in) ↔ 60–90cm (24–36in)
COOK'S NOTES Good for rich stews and pasta dishes.

◀ POT MARJORAM
Origanum onites
❄❄☼
This variety will grow as a perennial when planted in full sun. Allow the soil to dry before watering. This has a less sweet, more piquant flavour than other varieties.
HABIT Small, shrubby
↕ 30–60cm (12–24in)
↔ 30–60cm (12–24in)
COOK'S NOTES Rub on meats before roasting, add to pasta, or sprinkle on cheese, egg, and vegetable dishes.

The aromatic leaves form a pretty, dense mat in winter

SWEET MARJORAM ▲
Origanum majorana
❄☼
The curving stems don't grow as tall as those of common oregano, and the leaves have a more delicate, sweet flavour. Mulch with straw to prevent stems lolling.
HABIT Shrubby
↕ 30–60cm (12–24in) ↔ 30–60cm (12–24in)

Round, fuzzy leaves release milder aromas and flavours

DITTANY OF CRETE ▶
Origanum dictamnus
❄❄☼
Short stems produce woolly-looking leaves that are unlike other oreganos and have a milder aroma and flavour. The arching stems look best in hanging baskets or elevated pots.
HABIT Low growing
↕ 20cm (8in) ↔ 30–60cm (12–24in)
COOK'S NOTES Used to make tea in Crete. It is good with grilled fish.

SCENTED GERANIUM
Pelargonium spp.

Despite their common name, pelargoniums are not related to true geraniums; instead they are perennial herbs with woody stems. Some of these have edible leaves, which have a variety of aromas.

❄ ☼

GROW Plant young plants or cuttings in good garden soil enriched with compost in full sun in spring, once all risk of frost has passed. The plants die back in frost, so it is a good idea to plant them in pots that can be moved indoors in cold weather. Pinch out faded blossoms to encourage new blooms. Take cuttings in autumn.
HARVEST Pick individual leaves from plants any time during the growing season.
COOK Use the leaves to flavour preserves, syrups, teas, butters, and sorbets. As with bay, remove the leaves before serving.

The leaves of this variety have the most delicate scent

LEMON-SCENTED GERANIUM ▶
Pelargonium crispum
Its divided leaves release a lemon aroma when crushed. Keep well watered during hot, dry spells.
HABIT Upright, neat
↕ 30–90cm (12–36in)
↔ 30–90cm (12–36in)

PRINCE OF ORANGE GERANIUM ▶
Pelargonium 'Prince of Orange'
Produces orange-scented, green, crinkled leaves. Pretty in herb gardens and at the front of ornamental borders. Pinch tips to promote bushy growth.
HABIT Upright, leafy
↕ 30–90cm (12–36in)
↔ 30–90cm (12–36in)

ROSE-SCENTED GERANIUM ▲
Pelargonium graveolens
Very finely divided leaves. There are many rose-scented geraniums, but this one has the softest scent of all. Give a mid-summer feeding of liquid fertilizer.
HABIT Upright, leafy
↕ 30–90cm (12–36in) ↔ 30–90cm (12–36in)
COOK'S NOTES Good for lining cake tins as an alternative, fragrant baking parchment. Infuse to make rose-scented syrup.

PARSLEY
Petroselinum spp.

One of the most useful herbs, bearing nutritious leaves packed with flavour. This biennial is good in pots and makes an attractive edging plant.

❀❀☼☼

GROW This herb blooms in the second year, but the seed needs sowing in spring each year to produce plants in succession. Parsley favours rich, well-drained garden soil and a sunny or partially shaded spot. Enrich the soil around the plant with compost in mid-summer.

HARVEST Select whole stems, leaving plenty on each plant so they stay well nourished.

COOK Both the stems and leaves can be added to a multitude of savoury dishes; from omelettes to stews to baked fish. Parsley freezes well but is not worth drying.

The delicate-looking leaves have a strong flavour

FLATLEAF PARSLEY ▼
Petroselinum crispum var. *neapolitanum*
Soak seed in warm water for 24 hours before planting to hasten germination. It has a more pronounced flavour than the curly type.
HABIT Neat, bushy
↕ 60–90cm (24–36in)
↔ 30–60cm (12–36in)

Sprigs look pretty as a garnish

▲ CURLY PARSLEY
Petroselinum crispum
If starting from seed, expect germination to take up to a month. It has a mild flavour.
HABIT Low-growing mound
↕ 25–30cm (10–12in) ↔ 30cm (12in)
COOK'S NOTES Chop finely if sprinkling on dishes as an edible garnish, as the tough curly leaves can be rough on the palate.

ANISE
Pimpinella anisum

The leaves of this annual can be used as flavouring, but it is the seeds that are most prized for their rich, liquorice flavour.

GROW Anise has a tap root and resents moving once established, so in spring, sow seed in a light, well-drained soil in full sun where you want it to grow. It takes about four months from seedling to seed-bearing, so it's not for regions that have late frosts or prolonged cold weather. Water infrequently but deeply.

HARVEST Just before the seeds ripen, cut the stalks and hang them to dry in paper bags (see p116).

COOK Chop fresh leaves to add a spiced sweetness to salads and fruit; seeds enhance breads, apple pies, curries, fish stews, cakes, and dried fruit dishes.

HABIT Upright, leafy
‡ 50cm (20in) ↔ 24–45cm (10–18in)

PURSLANE
Portulaca oleracea

This annual makes a good pot herb, or you can use the leaves, stems, and flower buds to add a mangetout-like flavour and texture to salads.

GROW Sow seed in any soil in full sun in spring. Purslane grows quickly once the ground warms up. If harvesting the herb from fields, make sure no pesticides have been used. It does require some additional water in hot summers.

HARVEST Pull up whole plants any time before the flower buds open.

COOK Its flower buds, stems, and fleshy leaves make a good ingredient in mixed salads. You can cook the foliage as you would spinach, or chop them and add to tabbouleh.

HABIT Trailing
‡ 20–45cm (8–18in) ↔ 45–60cm (18–24in)

Purslane is believed to be a rich source of omega-3 fatty acids

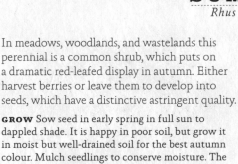

SUMAC
Rhus spp.

In meadows, woodlands, and wastelands this perennial is a common shrub, which puts on a dramatic red-leafed display in autumn. Either harvest berries or leave them to develop into seeds, which have a distinctive astringent quality.

GROW Sow seed in early spring in full sun to dappled shade. It is happy in poor soil, but grow it in moist but well-drained soil for the best autumn colour. Mulch seedlings to conserve moisture. The suckers from this shrub can be invasive.

HARVEST Cut off dense clusters of red-berried seed heads in the autumn. Plant a few seeds directly and store the rest in paper bags.

COOK Use the seed heads whole, ground, or extract the juice after soaking to add a pleasantly sour, fruity flavour to Middle Eastern dishes. Dried seed heads make a calming tea and are also good scattered over flat bread dough before baking.

STAGHORN SUMAC ▶
Rhus typhina
✹✹✹☼☀
The branches are covered with downy hairs, hence its common name.
HABIT Upright, bushy
↕ 1.8–2.1m (6–7ft) ↔ 90cm–1.2m (3–4ft)
COOK'S NOTES Its berries can be washed, strained, sweetened, and made into pink lemonade.

SICILIAN SUMAC ▼
Rhus coriaria
✹✹☼
Grow it only in full sun in dry or moist soil. This variety has the best flavoured, tart berries of all the sumacs.
HABIT Upright, open, branching
↕ 3m (10ft) ↔ 1.5–1.8m (5–6ft)
COOK'S NOTES Its acidic berries are made into a condiment in the Middle East.

The smoke from burning seed heads is used by beekeepers to calm bees

BLACKCURRANT
Ribes nigrum

The black fruits of this bushy, deciduous shrub have a slightly tart flavour and are a great source of vitamin C.

✿✿✿☼

GROW Plant young plants in a sunny part of the herb garden in good, well-drained soil. They are happy in cold winter areas. Mulch each shrub with rich compost in the spring before the buds form.
HARVEST Pick the ripe berries in mid-summer.
COOK Blackcurrants are a perfect ingredient for ice cream, summer puddings, jams, preserves, cordials (see p175), and liqueurs.

HABIT Bushy shrub
↕ 1.2–1.5m (4–5ft) ↔ 1.2–1.5m (4–5ft)

ROSE
Rosa rugosa

This is the perfect rose for the herb garden. This perennial produces fragrant blooms followed by large, tomato-red hips (seed pods).

✿✿✿☼

GROW Plant young plants in full sun in decent soil next to a fence, wall, trellis, or other support. This rose has good pest and disease resistance.
HARVEST Pick flowers as needed, but leave some to develop into hips. Collect the hips when they have reached a good size and have turned red.
COOK Use newly opened flowers to make rosewater and the flowers or hips to make syrup. Dried petals are ground for use in spice blends.

HABIT Rambling
↕ 1–2m (3–6ft) ↔ 1–2m (3–6ft)

Do not deadhead after flowering, to allow hips to develop

SORREL
Rumex spp.

This leafy herb adds a tangy, acidic flavour to soups and rich foods. There are two species and both are perennials that grow easily from seed.

✳✳✳☀

GROW Sow seed in rich, moist soil in a partially shaded spot; the leaves become bitter in full sun. Sorrel is quick to bolt, so remove flower stalks to encourage leaf growth.

HARVEST Pick leaves throughout the growing season while they are young. The leaves freeze well.

COOK Use fresh leaves in salads, sauces, soups, and in fish dishes. Sorrel is the perfect partner for butter and cream. Mature leaves can be acidic so are best used in moderation.

The smaller, shield-shaped leaves have a succulent texture

GARDEN SORREL ▶

Rumex acetosa

The common variety of sorrel makes a clump of tangy, sharp-flavoured leaves that can be divided in autumn.

HABIT Clump-forming, low growing

↕ 60–90cm (24–36in)

↔ 90cm–1.2m (3–4ft)

Sharp in flavour, the large dark leaves partner rich foods perfectly

◀ FRENCH SORREL

Rumex scutatus

This variety can take more sun than garden sorrel. The leaves have a milder, more lemony flavour and a succulent texture.

HABIT Clump-forming, low growing

↕ 15–25cm (6–10in)

↔ 60–90cm (24–36in)

ROSEMARY
Rosmarinus officinalis spp.

These perennials come in different shapes and sizes; from tall upright ones to those that hug the ground. The edible flowers can be blue, white, and, rarely, pink. All have needle-like aromatic leaves with a sweet, resinous smell.

GROW Sow seed or plant cuttings in pots or in the garden in spring. Rosemary tolerates poor, dry soil, but it thrives in good soil. Do not overwater; rosemary will die in boggy or wet soil.

HARVEST Cut off the outer stems and pick flowers as needed.

COOK A quintessential flavour of Mediterranean cooking. Cut sprigs for casseroles or as skewers to barbecue food. Chop leaves or use them whole with meat, especially lamb, casseroles, potatoes, fish, rice, and breads, or infuse in vinegar and oil. Flowers have a milder flavour and look good in ice cubes.

ROSEMARY ▶
Rosmarinus officinalis
✿✿☼
The common evergreen shrub has dark green, aromatic leaves.
HABIT Upright, bushy
↕ 1.5m (5ft) ↔ 1.5m (5ft)

The stems have a strong flavour and a woody texture, so remove cooked sprigs before serving dishes

◀ PROSTRATE ROSEMARY
Rosmarinus officinalis Prostratus Group
✿✿☼
A cascading form that will trail attractively over walls, down banks, and from hanging baskets. It has highly aromatic, strongly flavoured leaves. Renew by division every few years to prevent dead centres.
HABIT Trailing
↕ 25–60cm (10–24in)
↔ 1.2–2.4m (4–8ft)

ROSEMARY 'MAJORCA PINK' ▶
Rosmarinus officinalis 'Majorca Pink'
❄☼

Tall branches flop into an interesting shape when the plant matures. Carries lilac-pink flowers and a fruity fragrance. Ideal for pots, then it can be moved under cover in winter.
HABIT Upright
↕ 60cm–1.2m (2–4ft) ↔ initially 60cm–1.2m (2–4ft) but makes a 90cm–1.2m (3–4ft) mound when mature
COOK'S NOTES Use young sprigs to flavour olive oil, or to infuse milk, cream, or syrup.

Closely-packed leaves result in a bushy plant

ROSEMARY 'CORSICAN PROSTRATE' ▶
Rosmarinus officinalis 'Corsican Prostrate'
❄☼

This variety has arching stems and deep blue flowers, and spreads by creeping roots.
HABIT Arching
↕ 30–45cm (12–18in) ↔ indefinite
COOK'S NOTES Good when in flower as a garnish for leg or rack of lamb.

ROSEMARY 'MISS JESSOPP'S UPRIGHT' ▶
Rosmarinus officinalis 'Miss Jessopp's Upright'
❄❄☼

Slender stems and excellent flavour for culinary uses. Place at the rear of the herb garden in a sunny spot.
HABIT Upright, bushy
↕ 1.2–1.8m (4–6ft)
↔ 75–90cm (30–36in)

The blue flowers make an attractive garnish

◀ ROSEMARY 'TUSCAN BLUE'
Rosmarinus officinalis 'Tuscan Blue'
❄❄☼

Very tall, slender, aromatic plant that eventually turns bare at the base. A more cold-hardy variety, but wrap stems in frost-prone areas.
HABIT Upright
↕ 1.8–2.1m (6–7ft) ↔ 30–60cm (12–24in)

SAGE
Salvia spp.

Variegated leaves in sage plants tend to have a milder flavour

This perennial herb family is huge, but most of its members are ornamental, apart from these key culinary ones. Its crinkled, musky leaves can be used fresh or dried.

GROW Sages like the warm, dry soils of their native Mediterranean. Sow seed or plant young plants in a part of the herb garden where you have dug sand into the soil for good drainage. Sage needs no special care but does require watering if the soil becomes too dry. Take cuttings in summer.

HARVEST Pick individual leaves as needed, or take whole stems for bouquet garni (see p128).

COOK Raw, fresh leaves are a little hairy and have a strong flavour, so chop them very finely and use in small amounts. Add towards the end of cooking to give a distinctive taste to risotto, and pork, veal, and venison dishes; dried leaves are good for stuffings and with poultry, fish, potatoes, and carrots. You can use flowers to make summer teas.

GOLDEN SAGE ▶
Salvia officinalis 'Icterina'
❋ ❋ ☼
Golden variegations of green leaves make this a great garnish. Boost its mild flavour by planting it in full sun.
HABIT Upright
↕ 60cm (24in) ↔ 60cm (24in)

The leaves of this subtropical sage smell distinctly of pineapples

PINEAPPLE SAGE ▲
Salvia elegans

❀ ☼

This variety has slender, brittle stems with narrow, pineapple-scented leaves. It likes good, moist soil and may need support where growth is lush, and some frost protection.
HABIT Branching
↕ 90cm–1.2m (3–4ft) ↔ 30–60cm (12–24in)
COOK'S NOTES Its scarlet flowers are good for salads.

▲ PURPLE SAGE
Salvia officinalis 'Purpurascens'

❀ ❀ ☼

Less potent than the common sage, but with an attractive spicy note in its flavour.
HABIT Low growing
↕ 30–45cm (12–18in)
↔ 45–60cm (18–24in)

COMMON SAGE ▼
Salvia officinalis

❀ ❀ ☼

This is the best-known sage for culinary use. The oval leaves are highly aromatic and slightly spicy.
HABIT Low growing
↕ 30–45cm (12–18in)
↔ 60cm (24in)

◀ THREE-COLOUR SAGE
Salvia officinalis 'Tricolor'

❀ ❀ ☼

The leaf centres are green, but the margins run between pink and cream to striking effect. Full sun intensifies the colour changes. It has a mild flavour.
HABIT Upright
↕ 30–60cm (12–24in) ↔ 60cm (24in)

ELDER
Sambucus spp.

White flowers and small purple-black berries with a sweet muscat flavour are produced in profusion by this perennial. Both are used in cooking and for flavouring.

✻✻✻☼

GROW Sow seed in spring outdoors, or plant young plants in semi-shade and good, moist soil. Mulch with shredded leaves in autumn. Take hardwood cuttings in autumn.
HARVEST Pick flower heads in early summer and strip flowers off the stems. Harvest berries late in the season when they are purple-black. The berries are mildly poisonous when unripe and should not be eaten raw.
COOK Add flowers to drinks, cordials, custards, ice cream, and fruit desserts, particularly gooseberry fools and jelly. Brew dried flowers for tisanes. Use berries in jellies and for wine.

Berries are mildly poisonous when raw

EUROPEAN ELDER (BLACK ELDER) ▼
Sambucus nigra
This variety is most commonly found in Europe, hence its common name. Plant where you need a windbreak or to screen a herb garden.
HABIT Upright, shrubby
↕ 4.5–6.1m (15–30ft)
↔ 3–4.5m (10–15ft)

▲ **AMERICAN ELDERBERRY**
Sambucus canadensis
Grows wild in cold-winter areas of eastern North America. Prune to keep plants well behaved in the herb garden.
HABIT Shrubby, upright
↕ 3–3.6m (10–12ft) ↔ 3–3.6m (10–12ft)

Do not eat the leaves, as they are purgative

SALAD BURNET
Sanguisorba minor

This perennial is a pretty addition to a herb garden. Its toothed leaves are delicious in salads, imparting a cucumber-like taste.

❋❋❋☼◐

GROW Sow seed in spring in pots or in the garden. Salad burnet likes good garden soil and full sun to light shade. Pinch out flower buds and cut the leaves regularly to encourage new foliage.
HARVEST As it is an evergreen plant, you can clip leaves as needed year round.
COOK Add fresh leaves to mixed leaf salads.

HABIT Rosette forming
↕ 30cm (12in) ↔ 45–60cm (18–24in)

STEVIA
Stevia rebaudiana

The sugary tasting leaves of this perennial herb are 30–45 times sweeter than granulated sugar and have almost no calories.

❋❋❋☼

GROW Plant cuttings in acid soil in full sun in early summer. Sow seed indoors in late winter or early spring under cover and plant out when risk of frost has passed. Stevia requires a lot of water, so water deeply twice a week in the growing season.
HARVEST Pick individual leaves.
COOK Use the leaves fresh, dried, or ground, or boil them to make a syrup which can be used as a sugar substitute to sweeten puddings, fruit, and drinks.

HABIT Upright, bushy
↕ 45cm (18in) ↔ 45cm (18in)

The serrated leaves have a sugary flavour and a liquorice aftertaste

SAVORY
Satureja spp.

Plant both the perennial winter and annual summer savory in a herb garden and you can harvest their bitter, thyme-like leaves from spring until early winter.

GROW In spring, sow seed of both varieties in well-drained soil, or grow winter savory from cuttings. Enrich the soil with compost before planting and top-dress winter savory in pots.

HARVEST The leaves of summer savory have the most potency just before flowering. Winter savory is evergreen in all but very frosty regions, so it can be harvested any time.

COOK The fresh leaves of both varieties taste best young, but they keep their flavour when dried. Use sparingly in stuffings with other herbs. Good with veal and beans, peas, or other pulses.

As it is evergreen, winter savory leaves can be harvested year round

◀ WINTER SAVORY
Satureja montana

✳ ✳ ✳ ☼

Plant this variety in full sun. It has a coarser, stronger flavour.
HABIT Dwarf, bushy
↕ 30–38cm (12–15in) ↔ about 60cm (24in)

SUMMER SAVORY ▲
Satureja hortensis

✳ ✳ ☼ ☼

This makes a good pot plant. Plant in partial shade in hot gardens.
HABIT Open, upright with trailing stems
↕ 45cm (18in) ↔ 45cm (18in)
COOK'S NOTES It is most often used in bean dishes.

ALECOST
Tanacetum balsamita

British brewers have flavoured ales with this perennial herb since the Middle Ages. A few of its minty, sweet leaves go a long way in cooking.

❋❋❋☼

GROW Sow seed indoors or divide roots and plant out in well-drained soil enriched with compost in a sunny spot. Give plants adequate water during the growing season. Cutting back stems to 22–30cm (9–12in) forces more pretty, scalloped basal leaves.

HARVEST Pick individual leaves from mid-summer into autumn.

COOK Add fresh young leaves to salads, soups, stuffings, and cakes. Use leaves and flowers to make home-brewed beer.

HABIT Mat-forming, open
↕ 90cm (36in) ↔ 45cm (18in)

Leaves have a bitter tang, so use sparingly

DANDELION
Taraxacum officinale

This annual plant needs no introduction. If it appears in your garden, harvest the leaves, for they make delicious bitter spring salad greens.

❋❋❋☼☼

GROW This herb grows anywhere, but if it's not already in your garden, gather the seed from frothy seed heads in fields and lawns – but not too much. It needs no help to establish itself, other than a puff of breath to blow its seeds aloft. It will grow again from a tiny piece of root left in the soil.

HARVEST Gather the young leaves in early spring from your garden or places you know haven't been sprayed with herbicides or pesticides.

COOK Add fresh young leaves to salads, cook stems and larger leaves, which can be more bitter, and use petals in salads or to make wine.

HABIT Low-growing rosettes
↕ 30cm (12in) ↔ 45cm (18in)

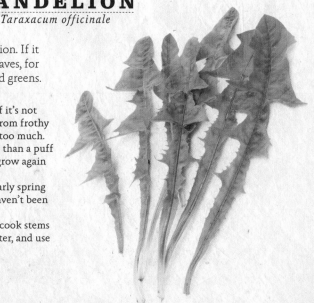

THYME
Thymus spp.

An essential addition to any herb garden. For a small plant, the leaves of this evergreen perennial have a curiously strong flavour. Bees love thyme's white to lilac flowers.

✿✿✿☼

GROW Sow seed in pots in spring (it may take a month for them to germinate, so be patient) or plant softwood cuttings. Thyme likes well-drained sandy soil and doesn't require a lot of water. In very hot climates, plant in semi-shade. Clumps can be divided in late spring.

HARVEST Clip stems as you need them to keep the plant from becoming woody and sparse.

COOK Add to any savoury dish or use to make bouquets garnis to flavour poultry, pork, and fish dishes, or to add to stuffings and vegetables. The leaves lose little of their flavour when dried.

A strong lemony flavour makes this perfect for cooking

▲ CARAWAY THYME
Thymus herba-barona
The dark green leaves have a distinctive caraway scent.
HABIT Low-growing, mat-forming
↕ 5–10cm (2–4in) ↔ 60cm (24in)
COOK'S NOTES Particularly good with stir-fries and meat.

◀ LEMON THYME
Thymus x *citriodorus*
This is a very good thyme for cooking, as the leaves have a strong citrus aroma.
HABIT Upright
↕ 30cm (12in) ↔ 60cm (24in)
COOK'S NOTES Perfect partner for chicken and fish dishes.

◄ **ORANGE-SCENTED THYME**
Thymus x *citriodorus* 'Fragrantissimus'
Use the spicy orange-scented leaves of this variety as a flavouring in place of orange peel.
HABIT Upright
‡ 30cm (12in) ↔ 20cm (8in)

This bushy, sturdy plant produces stems with plenty of flavour-packed leaves

▲ **COMMON THYME**
Thymus vulgaris
Give this variety a spot in full sun for the best flavour. It is the best-known thyme and the one most often used.
HABIT Compact, bushy
‡ 45cm (18in) ↔ 45cm (18in)
COOK'S NOTES Use in stews and casseroles.

SILVER THYME ►
Thymus vulgaris 'Argenteus'
Crushing the silver-grey and green variegated leaves will release their rich aroma.
HABIT Upright
‡ 30cm (12in) ↔ 30cm (12in)

Pretty grown in between paving, the aromatic leaves will withstand being trodden on

WILD CREEPING THYME ►
Thymus serpyllum
A more mildly scented variety, but still good for culinary use and aesthetically a real joy to have in the garden.
HABIT Low-growing, mat-forming
‡ 2.5–7.5cm (1–3in)
↔ 90cm (36in)

FENUGREEK
Trigonella foenum-graecum

Once used as animal fodder by the Greeks (its name means Greek hay), this annual herb has bitter leaves and maple-syrup-flavoured seeds.

❀❀❀☼

GROW Sow seed in a sunny spot in good garden soil in late spring when the soil is thoroughly warm. It needs adequate water during the growing season.
HARVEST Pick leaves any time during the growing season. Collect seed pods when they ripen in the autumn and dry them.
COOK Used by cooks in the Middle East and India, but less so in Europe or North America. Cook the bitter leaves in curries, use the seeds as a spice, and eat home-sprouted seeds in salads in small amounts.

HABIT Small, upright
↕ 60cm (24in) ↔ 30–45cm (12–18in)

The leaves of fenugreek resemble those of clover

NASTURTIUM
Tropaeolum majus

This annual vine rambles over supports bearing yellow, orange, and red flowers. The leaves, seeds, and flowers all have a spicy, peppery taste.

❀❀❀☼

GROW Sow seed in spring in good, rich soil in a sunny spot where you have plenty of space. Water well during the hot summer months.
HARVEST Pick leaves and flowers to use fresh in summer, and pick the seed pods just before they turn from green to brown.
COOK Add the colourful flowers and the peppery leaves to salads, and the unripe seeds to sauces and dressings.

HABIT Climbing (bush types available)
↕ 1.8–2.4m (6–8ft) ↔ 30cm (12in)

SWEET VIOLET
Viola odorata

The sweetly scented flowers of this perennial have long been used in perfumes and cookery. The leaves and flowers taste of Parma violets.

❀❀❀🌢☼☀

GROW Violets are natural denizens of woodlands and shady areas but will tolerate full sun in cool climates. Sow seed or bulblets in a suitable spot in your garden and they will spread themselves with abandon. Snip off tops after the frosts, then fertilize with a top dressing of compost early in the spring.
HARVEST Pick the little fragrant violet flowers as they appear. Harvest the milder-tasting leaves throughout the summer, as needed.
COOK Use the flowers in salads, to flavour drinks, as a colouring agent, and once crystallized, to decorate desserts. Add the leaves to salads.

HABIT Low-growing, clump-forming
↕ 15cm (6in) ↔ 30cm (12in)

Pretty purple flowers make a delicate garnish

A few leaves are palatable, but too many can cause digestive upset

GINGER
Zingiber officinale

This ancient perennial herb is a tropical one, but the edible roots can be successfully grown under cover in a temperate climate.

❀☼

GROW Buy cuttings or fresh roots in early spring and break them into 5-cm (2-in) pieces. Let the ends dry, then plant them just below the surface of a rich, moist soil. Ginger likes heat and humidity, so grow it in a pot that you can bring indoors in winter.
HARVEST After 3 months, dig up the plants. Discard the leaves and store the roots in moist kitchen towel in the salad drawer of the fridge for up to 3 weeks. It freezes well.
COOK Grate the root to add a refreshing tang to stir-fries, curries, biscuits, cakes, puddings, chocolate, and teas. Use frozen roots straight from the freezer.

HABIT Upright
↕ 1.5m (5ft) ↔ indefinite

Beneath delicate aromatic leaves lies a deliciously spicy edible root

GROW

Once you've chosen your herbs, it's time to
get growing. Find out how and where you
can sow seed or grow young plants, how
to keep them fed, watered, healthy, and
productive throughout the growing season,
and how to create new plants from old.

CLIMATE

Try to choose perennials that will thrive in your local climate. The symbols here (and in The Herb Catalogue) show a plant's ability to survive cold and wet climates and indicate, therefore, which conditions best enable these perennials to return each spring, or if herbs must be grown from seed each year.

❄ ❄ ❄ HARDY HERBS

These herbs can stay outside over winter in regions where temperatures drop to a minimum of -15°C (5°F) and the ground freezes solid, as they are adapted to survive in these conditions.
Five such plants are illustrated here.

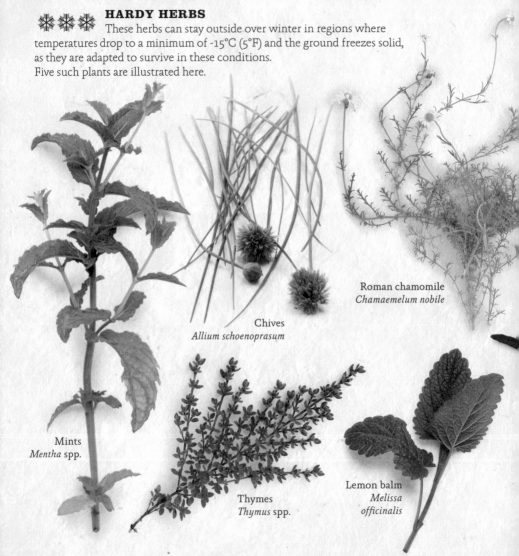

Roman chamomile
Chamaemelum nobile

Chives
Allium schoenoprasum

Mints
Mentha spp.

Thymes
Thymus spp.

Lemon balm
Melissa officinalis

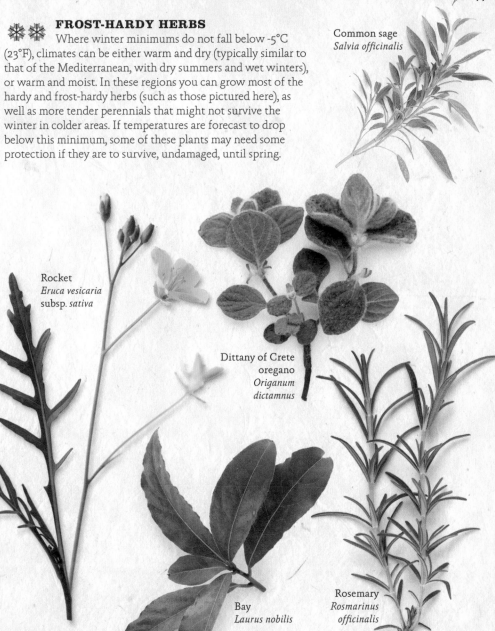

❄ ❄ FROST-HARDY HERBS

Where winter minimums do not fall below -5°C (23°F), climates can be either warm and dry (typically similar to that of the Mediterranean, with dry summers and wet winters), or warm and moist. In these regions you can grow most of the hardy and frost-hardy herbs (such as those pictured here), as well as more tender perennials that might not survive the winter in colder areas. If temperatures are forecast to drop below this minimum, some of these plants may need some protection if they are to survive, undamaged, until spring.

Common sage
Salvia officinalis

Rocket
Eruca vesicaria
subsp. *sativa*

Dittany of Crete
oregano
Origanum
dictamnus

Bay
Laurus nobilis

Rosemary
Rosmarinus
officinalis

❄ HALF-HARDY HERBS

These herbs can be killed by frosts and severe winter
weather, but they flourish where temperatures do not drop
below 0°C (32°F). Do not plant in frost pockets (areas where
cold air and frost collect). If frost is forecast, protect plants
such as those shown below with mulch, cover with cloches
or insulating fleece, or bring them indoors into a sunny spot.

Curry leaf
Murraya koenigii

Sweet
marjoram
*Origanum
majorana*

Chilli
peppers
Capsicum
spp.

Scented
geranium
Pelargonium
spp.

French
lavender
*Lavandula
dentata*

HERBS TOLERANT OF WET SOILS

Not many herbs like getting their feet wet, but there are a few (including those pictured here) that will tolerate damp soils. If you have a spot with constantly wet soil, try some of these herbs. All will do well in dappled shade, too.

Mints
Mentha spp.

Bergamot
Monarda didyma

Sweet violet
Viola odorata

Watercress
Nasturtium officinale

Meadowsweet
Filipendula ulmaria

PLANNING

Once you've identified your climate, it's time to choose where – or in what – to grow your herbs. Do you want to grow just a few herbs in pots, or would you like a more elaborate plot? Be mindful of how much sun your herbs need and position them appropriately in your garden.

POTS

Most culinary herbs take well to pot culture. Container growing can produce good results, as you can move plants around the garden to get the most sun or to give them some shade on very sunny days. It is also easier to move frost-tender plants indoors into a sunny spot during winter months. However, plants in pots also require frequent watering – daily in the summer. If you have a south-facing fence or wall, dress it up with a window box or wall-mounted pots spilling over with greenery. Window boxes allow you to grow a good selection of herbs in one space, and can be conveniently positioned by a kitchen window to make picking for cooking even easier. Plant herbs in generous containers with drainage holes in the bottom. Use fine compost mixed in equal quantities with vermiculite for the Mediterraneans, and 100 per cent potting compost for delicate herbs such as chervil or French tarragon.

INVASIVE HERBS

Some herbs can be invasive and take over the herb garden if left unchecked, so these are good candidates for planting in pots. These include:

• Mints *Mentha* spp.
• Bergamot *Monarda didyma*
• Lemon balm *Melissa officinalis*
• Mustard *Brassica* spp.
• Purslane *Portulaca oleracea*
• Lovage *Levisticum officinale*

Oregano *This herb will thrive in a pot and can easily be moved to a sheltered spot over winter.*

Use your space *Position pots against a south-facing wall in a sheltered spot to give them the best of the sun.*

Sharing space *Chives and other herbs make pretty and practical additions to vegetable beds.*

BEDS AND BORDERS

If you have already laid out a vegetable garden, or ornamental beds or borders, plant your culinary herbs between the plants that are already there. Position sun-loving herbs where they'll get lots of light, and tuck shade-lovers around taller ornamentals.

A small, informal, dedicated, culinary herb garden might occupy as little as 1.5 x 3.5m (5 x 12ft), but you can still pack in plenty of herbs. You do not need a path, as you will easily be able to reach all the plants from either side. If you have a choice as to where to put the herb garden, position it where you can see it best. It could also be planted within a larger vegetable garden.

A formal arrangement is possible even in the tiniest garden. In an ornamental herb garden or potager, you could plant low-growing herbs, such as Mother of Thyme or chamomile, between paths made of crushed rock, bricks, or flagstones.

Sketch out your dream garden on graph paper before you dig it. Then mark out planting areas in geometric or soft, curving patterns. If you add trellises, arbours, arches, pillars, water features, and statues you can give it a formal look. If you have a sloping garden, terraces make a beautiful addition.

PICK PLANTS FOR PLACES

No matter how tolerant a plant, there are some spots in the garden where plants simply don't thrive, so avoid panting anything there. Large trees and big, woody shrubs, for instance, commandeer all the available water and nutrients in their root zones.

Slopes drain quickly and are not suitable for moisture-loving herbs such as mints, but are an ideal place for drought-tolerant herbs such as lavender and rosemary. Low areas that remain constantly wet will rot the roots of all but bog-loving plants such as meadowsweet.

Beware of frost pockets (see p78) for plants that feel the cold – these will kill or shorten the growing season of less hardy herbs.

PLANT PARTNERS

Your herb garden will look its best when you match plants by following one simple rule: contrast. This works well both in the herb garden and when planting herbs within vegetable beds or ornamental borders.

Plant plants with small leaves, such as chervil or coriander, next to plants with large leaves, such as horseradish or even rhubarb. Juxtapose coloured leaves of red perilla and purple basil with green- or grey-leaved plants. Contrast the architecture of tall, thin plants such as fennel with low-growing mounds of lemon balm. You do not have to restrict yourself to herbs; add colour and excitement by interplanting flowers such as annual marigolds, ranunculus, petunias, and zinnias; or dramatic perennials such as perovskia and kniphofia.

Some woody herbs, such as bay and rosemary, can be trained as standards with a 60–90-cm (2–3-ft) stem and a ball of leaves on top. Standards are usually grown in generous pots that can be moved around the garden or patio to catch the sun. They look attractive when underplanted with low-growing herbs or annual flowers.

Bay tree
Underplant standards, such as bay, with other herbs to create a decorative display.

SOIL

In pots, it is easy to control the soil you use, but when planting into the garden you need to check your soil type. Garden soils are mostly loam, sandy, or clay. The best is loam, which is a combination of clay and sand. Clay is wet and heavy and needs compost and sand added to improve aeration; sandy soil is dry and light, and is only able to retain water and nutrients when you add compost to it.

TESTING SOIL
Try this simple test to discover the composition of your soil before planting your herb garden.

1 Take samples from three spots in the area where you want to grow herbs. Using a hand fork, remove any grass, weeds, or plants from the surface of the soil.

2 Push your spade down as deep as the blade will go and lift out a clod of earth. Repeat in two other places in your herb-garden patch.

3 Place the samples together in a paper bag and mix thoroughly, crumbling any clumps with your fingers. Discard any rocks that are larger than pea-sized.

4 Squeeze some soil in your palm and thump it with a finger. If it falls apart, it is loam; if it is gritty, it is sandy; if it forms a lump, as pictured, you have clay.

MAKING COMPOST

You can save yourself the expense of buying compost by making your own. Simply layer grass clippings, leaves, uncooked vegetable waste, and dead (but not diseased) plants into a compost bin that is 1.5m (5ft) square and 90cm (3ft) high. Do not add weeds or grass that have set seed. Farm-animal manure is an excellent addition – use one-sixth manure to one-part plant matter.

1 Collect your compostable material in a bin. Keep the heap moist and turn it every two weeks, using a fork or shovel, until the ingredients start to break down.

2 You can use your compost when it has turned dark brown in colour, is crumbling in texture, and looks and smells like soil.

PH LEVEL

Some herbs, such as angelica, prefer soil that is slightly acidic while others, such as thyme, favour alkaline soil, so it is a good idea to determine your soil's pH level. The pH level affects how plants get hold of the nutrients they need; most soil nutrients are available to plants in slightly acidic soils, about pH 6.8, but at either end of the scale nutrients become chemically locked up and unavailable. You can buy a simple test from your garden centre, then take a soil sample and add it to a test tube with the supplied solution. The indicator paper will reveal the pH of your soil.

GROWING FROM SEED

There are many advantages to growing herbs from seed. Home-sown herbs are cheaper than those bought from a nursery, and home-grown seedlings have healthy, garden-ready rootballs when the time comes to plant them out. Some herbs are best propagated in other ways, though (see pp90–1).

Some seeds are too small to be scarified using a knife or piece of sandpaper, so in this case use the edge of a nail file instead.

SCARIFYING SEED

If you are growing from seed, bear in mind that they all have different germination requirements; some may benefit from an overnight soak in water before planting in pots or in the garden, such as parsley, and a very few may need scarifying – a technique whereby you nick seeds with a knife or a piece of rough sandpaper to allow air and moisture in. Plants that need scarifying are those such as bay and coriander, that have hard hulls. Always follow the instructions on the seed packets for the individual cultivation requirements of the herbs and directions for sowing.

SOWING THE SEED

Sow seed into a plastic tray, a cellular tray, or into individual plastic or terracotta pots. Tap-rooted herbs do not like to be transplanted, so sow them in peat pots that can be planted out, pot and all.

1 Fill a pot with fine compost and gently firm it down. Water the soil and let it drain. Sow seed in dents or on the soil surface (according to the packet instructions).

2 Lightly cover the seed with vermiculite or more potting compost. Water again. Set the tray in a warm place and never let the compost dry out.

TRANSPLANTING

As seedlings develop they need more space to grow. Transplant them into individual or bigger pots (about 15-cm (6-in) pots are big enough, or go one size up from the pot they are already in), when they have formed four or more true leaves above the seed leaves.

HARDEN OFF

When all risk of frost is past, start to acclimatise, or harden off, transplanted plants to outdoor temperatures. Put seedlings outside during the day, uncovered, and bring them in at night. After a week or so, you can plant them or leave them out.

1 Remove the seedlings carefully from their container, gently pulling them out by holding the true leaves, not the stem, while lightly squeezing the bottom of the pot.

2 Make a hole with your finger in a pot of fresh compost to the depth of the seedling's rootball, then gently lower in the seedling to the same level as it was planted before.

3 Once the seedling is in position, backfill around the rootball of the plant with more compost and gently firm it down around the roots.

4 Water the plant well, label it, and position it in a warm, bright spot out of direct sunlight until it is mature enough to plant into its final position.

GROWING YOUNG PLANTS

Sometimes it may not be practical to raise plants from seed yourself, especially if you only want to grow a handful of different plants and don't have space to sow lots of seedlings, or if a plant is hard to grow from seed. Garden centres have a good selection, but nurseries have a broader range.

PICK A PERFECT PLANT

Do not buy plants with obvious problems or diseases, such as leaves with yellow veins or mildew. Herbs should have bright, sturdy stems and foliage, but knock the plant out of its pot and check the roots too; they should be healthy and plentiful and not fighting for space (see below). Check plants for live insects; you do not want to bring a problem home.

Leaves should have a good, healthy colour

Compost should be moist and free of weeds

Plants should have sturdy stems

Check the roots for pest damage and to see if they are potbound

GET TO THE ROOT OF THE PROBLEM

Vigorous leaves and stems do not always mean the plant is disease free; sometimes problems lie beneath the soil. Roots are the lifeline of plants, so it is important that they are healthy.

GOOD The plant should easily lift out of its pot and the roots should be plentiful but not overcrowded, with plenty of compost visible.

BAD Tease out and thin overcrowded roots before planting out in good soil. Check for root weevils and grubs.

POTTING ON

If you want to grow your herb in a pot, replant it when you get home in a pot one size bigger than it is in. You will need to repeat the process when your plants outgrow their new pots.

1 Make sure the new pot has a drainage hole, and place a handful of gravel in the bottom. Half-fill with potting compost and remove the plant from its pot.

2 Set the plant in the new pot and fill the space around the rootball with potting compost, firming it in gently as you go. Water the plant well.

PLANTING INTO THE GARDEN

Young plants bought from a nursery should be big enough to plant outdoors in the garden immediately. Plant them out as soon as you can to allow their roots to establish.

1 Prepare the soil by digging compost into the top 15–30cm (6–12in) of soil until the soil becomes loose and friable. Dig a generous hole in the prepared soil.

2 Place the plant in the hole to the depth it was in its pot. Backfill with soil around the plant and firm it in with the palms of your hands. Water the plant well.

PROPAGATING

Once plants are established, you can increase their number, or grow insurance plants in case some do not survive winter, by various propagating methods. See the individual entries in The Herb Catalogue for the best technique to use.

STEM CUTTINGS

You can take cuttings from stems at different times of the year. Take softwood cuttings from young, flexible stems in spring, semi-ripe ones from ripening, stiffening stems in late summer, and hardwood ones from stems that are turning woody at the end of the growing season.

I Select a healthy, non-flowering stem with mature leaves, such as this rosemary. Cut the stem at an angle just above the leaf attachment. Strip the lower leaves.

2 Cut the stem straight across, 5cm (2in) below the last leaf. Plant vertically in a pot of compost. Water well. Cover the pot with a clear plastic bag to retain moisture.

ROOT CUTTINGS

Make new plants from sections of semi-mature or mature roots of plants, such as mints and sweet cicely, when they are dormant (not growing), in mid- to late winter. Watercress is one exception to this rule, as root cuttings can be taken from it all year round.

I Lift the plant and tease the roots apart a little to find some good roots to use as cuttings – do not use any that are fibrous and immature.

2 Cut a 5-cm (2-in) piece; trim it straight across at the top and make a sloping cut at the base. Plant cuttings vertically in compost and cover with vermiculite.

LAYERING
This is a good method for propagating woody plants while stems are still attached to the plant.

1 In the dormant season, remove leaves from 10–50cm (4–20in) behind the tip of a flexible stem.

2 Add compost and sand where you will bury the stem. Peg the bent stem down towards the soil.

3 Cover the stem with soil, allowing the tip to protrude. Water well. In autumn, detach and pot up the plant.

DIVIDING PERENNIALS
Every three or four years, or when plants become too large, divide perennial herbs such as fennel.

1 Lift the entire plant using a garden fork and wash the soil off the rootball with a hose.

2 Take sections from the perimeter of the rootball, separating them by hand or with a sturdy knife.

3 Replant the crowns in good garden soil and water in well. Discard the woody central clump.

DIVIDING BULBS
Bulbous plants, such as garlic, produce bulblets which you can detach to create new plants.

1 Lift bulbs in autumn when the top growth has yellowed. Separate the bulblets around the base of the bulb.

2 Replant the bulblets in pots of fresh, moist compost to a depth of twice their length.

3 Cover the bulblets with fresh compost and water well. Grow until well established, then plant out.

FEEDING AND WATERING

Herbs grown in pots and those grown in the ground have different requirements. The individual entries in The Herb Catalogue list specific wants and needs, but these general guidelines will keep all plants healthy.

WATERING HERBS IN BEDS

If you are planting a selection of herbs in the garden you cannot always cater for individual preferences, but plants will usually tolerate shared conditions, as long as they have moist, well-drained soil. Work lots of compost into the soil to help it retain moisture and water it deeply when the top 5cm (2in) seems dry. The best time to water, if you are using an overhead sprinkler or watering can, is in the morning, so the sun has time to dry the leaves. Plants are most vulnerable to mildew and rot when they are wet during the night.

Water early Try to water your herbs in the morning.

FEEDING HERBS IN BEDS

Plants in open ground do not need much feeding because their roots travel to find the nutrition they require. However, you can give them a helping hand by spreading a 5-cm (2-in) layer of compost over the soil surface as a mulch over winter, then by digging it into the soil in spring to restore nutrients. Herbs that are harvested frequently during the growing season benefit from the occasional fertilizer feed in mid-summer too.

Homemade compost makes a good mulch

In a watering can, add granular or liquid fertilizer to water to feed herbs during the growing season. Follow the application instructions on the packet.

WATERING HERBS IN POTS

Plants in pots need to be watered more often than those in the ground, as their roots cannot travel as far to locate moisture. In hot summers you should water them every day, or install drip irrigation systems in each pot and set timers to automatically water them. You can help the soil to retain more water using special granules that absorb water and release it as and when needed.

1 Tip out some potting compost onto a flat surface and add a handful of the moisture-retaining granules.

2 Work the granules into the compost with your fingers so they are evenly mixed.

3 Half-fill the pot with the compost mix before planting your herb, then top up with more compost.

FEEDING HERBS IN POTS

Potted plants also need more attention than those in the ground when it comes to food. Ideally, you should feed potted herbs with fertilizer in granules or liquid form every 6 weeks throughout the growing season, especially if they are being regularly harvested.

Start feeding in spring when plants begin to produce new growth. It is also beneficial to scrape away the top 5cm (2in) of compost in the pot in spring and replace it with good, fresh compost. Stop feeding them in late summer, or you will encourage new growth when the plant should be slowing down before the dormant winter season.

Feed potted herbs with fertilizer in granules or in liquid form every 6 weeks during the growing season.

WEED CONTROL

Weeds compete with plants for water, sunlight, nutrients, and space, and if allowed to grow freely they will overwhelm the garden. The key to defeating weeds is to remove them as you see them. Make sure you remove all parts of them, including the root, to prevent regrowth.

BEATING WEEDS

Once the weeds start to appear in spring, you need to remove them by hand or with the help of a hand-fork where they have long roots. To help prevent them returning, remove weeds before they set seed and make sure you get as much of the root out of the soil as possible, particularly with perennial weeds. Check the soil regularly for any new shoots appearing and remove them immediately. If you want to clear a large area of weeds before planting in it, try either solarizing (see below) or using a mulch (see opposite).

Weeding by hand *This is the most effective way of removing all parts of weeds once they are established.*

SOLARIZING

This is a good method for clearing both small and large sections of soil of weeds. It is an organic technique, which kills weeds, bacteria, and nematodes in the soil before you plant.

In early summer, clear a patch of soil of any plants, weeds, or large stones, and level it off. Water it thoroughly until it is soaked, then cover the area with clear plastic sheeting and bury it at the edges to prevent air getting in or out. (Do not use black or coloured sheeting because they block the sun's rays; transparent sheeting allows the rays to penetrate and turn into sterilizing heat.) Over the next 6–8 weeks, the sun will create killing heat and steam under the plastic. After that time, remove the plastic and plant the herbs immediately, trying to disturb the soil as little as possible. Mulch the patch once you have planted out the herbs.

MULCHES

Laying down a 15-cm (6-in) mulch in spring just as new growth emerges will stop weed germination, but as it rots down the soil nitrogen level will deplete, so spread a 5-cm (2-in) layer of compost on the soil before mulching. Top with a mulch of your choice – it can be purely practical or more aesthetically pleasing. Pull up any weeds that find their way through the mulch.

Lay thick sections of newspaper on the soil above the plant's roots, leaving only a small space around the stem. Hold the paper down with stones.

Chipped or shredded bark makes a good mulch in its own right, or can be used to cover other less attractive mulches such newspaper or weed-suppressant matting.

For a neat and tidy mulch, place a 15–20-cm (6–8-in) layer of weed-seed-free compost on the soil and cover it with a good layer of gravel.

Weed-seed-free hay makes an attractive, effective, and nutritious mulch that will improve the soil and feed plants as it decays.

IMPROVING YOUR HARVEST

To keep the garden tidy and productive, some maintenance is required at different times of the year. A little pruning and deadheading goes a long way towards increasing your plants' productivity and ensuring that the harvest keeps coming, sometimes even into the winter months.

THE GROWING SEASON

Spring and summer are the times of year when growth is fastest, so maintenance during this growing season means more than just keeping the soil moist and pulling up weeds. You need to remove flowers from herbs whose leaves are used in cooking, as this forces the plants' energies into making new, leafy growth. Both perennial and annual herbs have a growth cycle that tends to shut down once it produces seed, so deadhead flowers and remove flower stalks to prevent plants going to seed. Keep an eye out for pests or diseases (see pp98–101), and for animal damage. If some stalks, stems, or leaves are yellowing, clip them off, as well as any dead or diseased tissue. If a herb is outgrowing its spot or crowding other useful plants, trim it back. Tie in climbing stems to trellis or supports as they appear.

REMOVE FLOWERS

Cut off flowers as they open during the growing season; it also promotes new blooms.

Using a pair of sharp, clean secateurs, cut back lavender and other flowering herbs after harvesting their blooms. Trim them to a neat shape.

PINCHING OUT

Removing the growing tips and developing flower buds encourages more leafy growth.

Using your thumb and forefinger, remove any developing flower buds or growing tips on herbs that you are growing for their leaves only.

CUT BACK OLD GROWTH

As the weather turns cold in autumn and winter, cut back any dying, yellowing growth. In early spring, hard prune perennial herbs such as lavender to encourage new growth and a neat shape.

1 Using secateurs, prune back old, dead wood to the point at which the plant is starting to regrow, such as where you can see new buds forming.

2 Leave 2.5–5cm (1–2in) of last season's growth and add a thick mulch to protect frost-tender plants from winter weather, if necessary.

CONTAINER CARE

Plants growing in containers have restricted space and a limited amount of soil, so these herbs do need special care. As well as supplementary feeding (see p93), add fresh compost to the pot halfway through the growing season to boost the soil's nutrient level, and water regularly throughout the growing season; daily in hot temperatures. Pot-grown plants benefit from repotting every now and again. So, every spring, check to see if potted plants have become root-bound, and if they have, repot them into new containers (see p88–9). However, if repotting isn't practical, just remove the plant from its pot, loosen tangled roots and prune back the rootball a little, remove 2.5cm (1in) of surface soil, then return it to its pot. Top up to just below the rim with fresh compost or good potting soil.

Herbs in containers benefit from constant harvesting to encourage new growth and to keep the plants under control in their restricted space.

PESTS

One of the virtues of many culinary herbs – especially Mediterranean herbs – is that the aromatic volatile oils they exude are produced by the plants primarily to ward off insects. So, many of the plants in your herb garden will naturally protect themselves against pests. However, here are a few to look out for.

LEAF MINERS
Tiny worms will bore through the tissues inside leaves, causing clearly visible, twisting white trails. The best control is to pick off and destroy infested leaves when you see them.

CATERPILLARS
Chewed leaves are the work of many pests but caterpillars are some of the worst offenders. Pick them off by hand several times weekly (wear a glove, as some have spines that can irritate skin), and dispose of them as you wish. You can also encourage native parasitic wasps to feast on them by planting flowering herbs that attract them, such as dill or sweet woodruff, or spray infested plants with a special homemade solution. (Whiz a peeled head of garlic with two cups of water and strain the liquid before use.)

Slugs Pillagers of young plants and fresh growth.

SLUGS AND SNAILS
The bane of all gardeners' lives, slugs and snails chew on young seedlings or new fresh growth and leave little to crop. There are many theories about how best to control them. If you are an organic gardener you can use slug traps – these are pots that have a little beer in the bottom and which are sunk into the soil alongside prized or particularly vulnerable plants. The snails and slugs are lured to the traps by the smell, fall in, and then drown. You need to empty the pots of dead creatures regularly and refill with beer. Alternatively, you can pick the slugs and snails off plants by hand, if you are prepared to venture out at night to do this, when they are most active. Again, the best control is to drown the insects; do not throw them over the fence, as they have a tendency to return. If you don't want to get this close to them, you could try the, non-toxic, organic pellets that are available.

SHORT, SHARP SHOCK
Apply copper tape just below the rim of pots or other containers to deter slugs and snails. This metallic tape gives them a mild electrical shock as they pass over it.

ROSEMARY BEETLES

Distinctive colourful markings make rosemary beetles easy to identify. They eat the leaves and tips of lavender, rosemary, sage, and thyme, causing serious damage. Pick them off by hand and destroy them as you see them.

VINE WEEVILS

A major pest, these grubs come out at night, mostly in spring and autumn, and chew notches out of leaf margins and devour roots. They are difficult to control biologically, but you can add nematodes to the soil to kill them.

Beautiful but deadly *Rosemary beetles destroy herbs.*

Night terrors *Nocturnal leaf- and root-eating grubs.*

APHIDS

These plant-sucking pests, along with scale, whitefly, mealy bugs, thrips, spittle bugs, and red spider mites, will weaken a plant's growth. Spritz them off plants as you see them with a forceful jet of water from a hose, or use an organic, insecticidal soap.

BAY SUCKER NYMPHS

If the edges of the leaves on your bay plant suddenly start to thicken, yellow, and curl, it may be suffering an infestation of this sap-sucking insect. Pick off the greenish brown, winged adults as you see them and remove and destroy any affected leaves.

Tiny suckers *Aphids drain the life from healthy herbs.*

Greedy nymphs *These cause leaves to thicken and curl.*

DISEASES

Most herbs are remarkably free of plant diseases, and many can be prevented by good care and maintenance when working among your plants, but occasionally diseases do develop. If you deal with them in good time, though, you can avoid any lasting damage to the plant.

AVOID DISEASES

Herbs are seldom attacked by bacterial and fungal diseases, and often prevention is the best cure. There are several ways in which you can protect your herbs. Grow resistant varieties and apply good cultural practices and hygiene in the garden. Do not feed plants as the autumn's cool weather sets in, as this stimulates weak growth. Try not to work in the garden when it is wet as you may inadvertently spread diseases. Sterilize your secateurs between cuts while pruning even healthy plants to prevent any latent diseases spreading or developing. Dip the blades into a solution that is 10 per cent bleach and 90 per cent water, then carefully wipe them dry using a clean cloth. Examine plants regularly and act quickly if you spot signs of disease. Remove infected leaves as they fall and do not leave them lying on the soil surface. Make sure that you dispose of any infected plant material carefully – preferably by burning it. Do not place it on the compost heap.

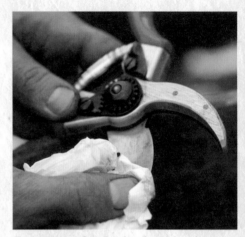

Keep secateurs clean *Sterilize them to prevent spreading infections around the herb garden.*

BACTERIA

Sometimes bacteria will enter the plant through wounds. If this happens you can treat the plant with a commercial spray or make your own organic version. Spray the affected plants with a mixture made from a dozen garlic cloves puréed in 1.2 litres (2 pints) of water and strained. If the plants do not respond within days, clip off and destroy the infected parts. Remember to sterilize your secateurs before you use them again.

Sprays *Use an organic spray to treat any bacterial diseases that affect your plants.*

FUNGI

This type of disease is fairly rare among herbs, although mint is prone to rust, and downy and powdery mildews can develop in humid, warm, and wet climatic conditions. There are organic controls for fungal diseases. Fungus prefers a slightly acid leaf surface, so spraying with an alkaline solution can prevent it taking hold. Spray with elemental sulphur, or Bordeaux mixture, or make your own solution. Mix 1 heaped tbsp of bicarbonate of soda with 1 tbsp of dormant oil (available at garden centres), ½ tsp of insecticidal soap (or washing-up liquid), in 4 litres (1 gallon) of lukewarm water. Spray when plants are young or seedlings show four true leaves. Reapply after rain. Do not use more than the recommended amount of bicarbonate of soda, as too much can defoliate plants.

Powdery mildew *A white fungus develops on leaves.*

VIRUSES

The varied symptoms of viral diseases make them difficult to identify. Among the most common are mosaic viruses, which cause white, yellow, or light green dots on leaves. Viruses often cause curled leaves, too, and ring spot viruses result in pale, yellowed ringed spots on leaves. Viruses do not cause any serious damage, but if you wish, pull up affected plants and destroy them.

Curled leaves *This can be a sign of a virus that has been transmitted by sucking insects or infected tools.*

Rust *Unsightly small brown patches of spores appear on the underside of leaves.*

HARVEST
AND STORE

There are a few golden rules to follow to
ensure you go on harvesting your herbs
for months. Besides cutting to use fresh,
harvest the leaves, flowers, seed heads, and
roots to store for use when fresh herbs
are not available after the growing season.

REAPING THE HARVEST

Herbs contain myriad culinary components. Besides the leaves, you can use the stalks, stems, flowers, seeds, berries, and even the root. At the end of the growing season, harvest and dry the whole plant to use throughout the winter.

HOW AND WHEN TO PICK

Harvesting various parts of herbs involves different techniques and timings to ensure you pick them when they are full of flavour. You can cut herbs for using fresh throughout the growing season, and even through the winter if they are evergreen. However, if you want to harvest leafy herbs for drying or to store, pick them in early summer when they have the most flavour – just before the flower buds open. Herbs produce their flavoursome volatile oils at night because the hot midday sun evaporates them each day, so the best time to harvest is in the early morning. Flowers appear from spring through summer and can be picked for use as they appear, but if you want the seeds for cooking, or for sowing the next year, leave the flower heads untrimmed. They will then set seed, ready to be cut down, dried, and stored in autumn.

Keep picking *Harvest little and often to encourage new, fresh growth*

DO'S

• Snip off stems and leaves early in the day, before the sun is at its strongest.

• Always use a sharp, clean knife or pair of secateurs or scissors.

• Harvest from all over the plant to keep it neat.

• Feed herbs with liquid fertilizer after making a substantial harvest.

DON'TS

• Avoid cutting into old, woody growth, as it may not re-grow.

• Do not use leaves and flowers that are damaged or discoloured; remove and discard them.

• Avoid deadheading flowers in late summer if you want to collect seeds in autumn.

• Do not scrub leaves vigorously – rinse and pat dry.

LEAVES

Leaves are the most commonly used part of
herbs. Take leaves from here and there all over
the plant rather than from one spot so the
plant keeps a neat, balanced shape.

Pinch off the tender sage leaves with their stalks at the
tips of their stems, either using scissors, secateurs, or
your thumb and forefinger.

STEMS

The stems are the main axis of the plant,
supporting leaves and flowers. In clump-forming
herbs, cut the stems 2.5cm (1in) above the soil level
to enable them to regrow.

Take stems *Harvest stems
of rosemary and strip off
the leaves between thumb
and forefinger (see p122)*

STALKS

Technically these are the stems of a leaf, but
sometimes, as with chives, they are also the
leaf itself. Never cut off chives completely.
This exhausts and damages the bulbs.

Chive spears *Take
individual spears
from here and there*

Keep it neat
*Cut individual
lavender stems to
keep the plant's shape*

FLOWERS

Cut off stems of small flowers such as lavender and meadowsweet using secateurs, or pick large blooms such as marigold by hand.

If you want only a few individual flowers, such as nasturtiums, pick them off the plant using your thumb and forefinger, taking as little stalk as possible.

SEEDS

Harvest seeds from anise, fennel, caraway (here), and coriander while still on the plant, or cut off stems with seed heads to dry (see p116).

Put a sheet underneath the plant from which you want to harvest seeds, then gently shake the seed heads over your hand. What you don't catch, the sheet will.

BERRIES

Most berries are ripe if they come away from the plants easily when gently tugged. Blackcurrants and elderberries can be carefully stripped from the stems using your fingers, or you can snip off the complete trusses and separate the berries from the stems back in the kitchen.

To harvest ripe blackcurrants, hold the stem between two fingers and run them down the length to strip off the berries into the palm of your other hand.

ROOTS

If harvesting during the growing season, expose roots of plants such as ginger and horseradish with a trowel, then cut portions of root from the mother plant with pruners or the sharp edge of a spade before replanting the roots. If you are lifting the whole plant in autumn to keep it indoors over the winter, wash off the soil and remove the stems then leave to dry off. Lay the whole, dry roots on sand in trays, cover with more sand, and store in a cool, dark place, such as a garage.

Using a trowel, carefully dig out the roots of the horseradish plant and lift them onto the soil surface, taking care not to damage them.

WHOLE PLANT

If you are using more than one section of a plant at a time, or you are cutting down plants at the end of the growing season to store, remove individual stems or flower stalks of clump-forming herbs such as lovage, angelica, fennel, lavender, lemongrass, salad burnet, and watercress. If it is during the growing season, do not take more than half the plant to allow it to regrow. Cut the stems just above the soil level. If you want the root, too, dig up the whole plant and harvest the parts individually.

To harvest complete stems from a plant, cut them off about 5cm (2in) above the soil level using secateurs.

SHORT-TERM STORAGE

Herbs are at their most fragrant and vibrantly flavourful straight from the garden. It's always best to pick what you need for a dish or a meal and use it immediately, but that may not always be convenient. However, there are a number of techniques that help keep herbs as "garden fresh" as possible. For use within hours of harvesting, keep them handy on the worktop. For use within a few days, prepare the herbs ahead and chill them.

On the worktop Delicate herbs such as tarragon, parsley, chervil, mint, oregano, or coriander keep well for a few days in a jug or vase of fresh water.

CHOPPED HERBS IN THE FRIDGE

Preparing chopped herbs ahead saves you time at the last minute. This is useful when you need a lot of fresh herbs, such as chives, mint, or basil, for several dishes, or you are cooking for a crowd.

1 Rinse, drain, and dry the whole herbs. Chop them finely (see p123) and place them in small dishes, ramekins, or mugs.

2 Cover with dampened kitchen paper and chill for up to 3 days. To store for an extra couple of days, cover with a layer of cling film.

WHOLE HERBS IN THE FRIDGE

Many herbs, such as basil, flatleaf parsley, chives, or tarragon can be chilled whole, but first rinse the herbs and pat them dry with kitchen paper or a clean towel.

I Dampen a sheet of kitchen paper. Gently squeeze out any excess water, and flatten. Moist kitchen paper will prevent the herbs from drying out.

2 Fold and then wrap the paper fairly loosely around the stems. Alternatively, you could wrap the moistened paper around the whole sprig.

3 Slip the wrapped herbs into a freezer bag and flatten it gently to remove some of the air. Seal the bag and chill in the fridge for up to a week.

Jars of herbs *You can also scrunch up the dampened kitchen paper and put it in a jar with sprigs of herbs. Seal with the lid and refrigerate.*

FREEZING

Most herbs keep their flavour extremely well during freezing but their appearance tends to suffer. Frozen herbs work well in salad dressings, sauces, stuffings, toppings, soups, and in slowly cooked dishes, such as roasts and pot roasts. You can freeze herbs in oil or water.

Flower cubes Pick edible flowers, such as borage, and freeze them individually in ice cube trays ready to use in drinks and to flavour syrups, custards, and jellies.

HERB OIL MIXES

Various herbs and garlic freeze well with a little olive oil. Freeze the herbs singly or combined with others, such as basil with garlic; garlic with grated root ginger and Thai basil; parsley with garlic, thyme, and oregano; or sage with fennel.

1 Coarsely chop the herbs in a food processor. Whiz briefly. With the motor running, add enough olive oil to lightly coat the herbs (about 1 tbsp oil to 3 tbsp herbs).

2 Spoon the mixture into very small freezer bags, seal them securely, label, and place in the freezer. Herbs in oil can be frozen for up to 4 months.

HERB ICE CUBES

Ice cube trays are an easy way to store chopped herbs, such as chives, parsley, tarragon, dill, chervil, coriander, or even welsh onions, in the freezer. Use them straight from frozen in hot liquids.

You can freeze finely chopped single herbs or herb combinations. Fill an ice cube tray to the brim with the herbs and pour water over just to cover. Freeze until solid, about 2 hours. Pop the frozen cubes out of the tray and slip a few at a time into freezer bags. Close, label, and place in the freezer until needed. Use within 6 months.

FROZEN GARLIC ROLL

Chopped herbs, singly or mixed, as well as garlic, can be shaped into a roll and frozen without having to add water or oil. They can then be added to your cooking straight from the freezer.

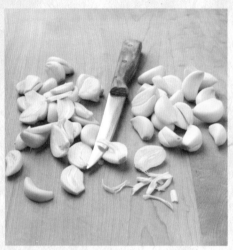

1 Peel and halve the cloves of 2 or 3 bulbs of very fresh garlic. Remove any green shoots in the cloves with the point of a knife and discard.

2 Using the side of a large chef's knife, smash the garlic cloves flat by pressing down quickly and firmly on the flat side of the blade with the palm of your hand.

3 Put the smashed cloves over the centre of a piece of cling film, keeping them well away from the edges.

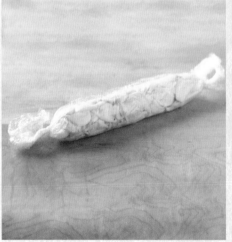

4 Bring up the long edges, and roll the cloves in the cling film to make a cigar shape. Twist the ends to seal. Place in the freezer.

5 To use, open up at one end and expose some of the garlic. Slice or shave off the amount you need. Reseal and return the roll to the freezer. Use within 4 months.

DRYING

Drying is an ideal way to preserve the flavour of herbs with woody stalks and tougher leaves, such as bay, thyme, and rosemary. Once dried, other herbs, such as mint and sage, taste noticeably different. Most home-dried herbs will, however, lose their flavour after six months as their essential oils evaporate.

DRYING FLAT

Individual leaves, fronds, and small spriglets of herbs, such as thyme, rosemary, marjoram, oregano, fennel, dill, bay, or sage, can be dried flat on a piece of muslin stretched over a frame. Place them out of direct sunlight in a dry, airy room, such as an attic, for at least 2 weeks until their colour fades a little and the herbs become slightly brittle.

1 Pluck the herbs from their stem into separate leaves or small clusters. Place them flat on the muslin in a single layer so they do not touch one another.

2 Once dry (leave for at least 2 weeks) pack the herbs loosely in clean glass jars with tightly fitting lids. Seal the jar and store away from direct light. Use within 4–6 months.

HANGING HERBS

Air circulates around herbs easily when they are hung to dry. Hang a few strips of unwaxed orange or lemon peel to dry on the line, too – their flavours mix well with dried herbs during cooking. Leave for at least 2 weeks until the colour fades a little and the herbs are brittle.

1 Make herb posies with 3–4 stems each of single herbs, such as bay, fennel fronds, rosemary, or thyme. Avoid using more than one herb in the same bundle, as different herbs have different drying times. Tie the bundles together with kitchen string.

2 Fix the bundles to a line in an airy, dry room out of direct sunlight. After at least 2 weeks untie the herbs and store them in sealed jars. Use within 4–6 months.

SEEDS

Fennel, dill, and coriander seeds, among others, can be home-dried for culinary use (and sowing). Dried seeds are best when used within 6 months before all their essential oils have evaporated.

1 Plants make seeds after they flower. Select a strong-looking plant that has gone to seed and harvest it by cutting the stems just above the soil line (see p107).

2 Bunch the stems together and tie them securely with string, leaving some extra for hanging them up. Hold the stems upside down to make sure they are secure.

3 Cover the seed heads with muslin (or a brown paper bag) and tie securely in place. Hang upside down in a dry, airy room out of direct sunlight.

4 After a week or so the seeds will drop off the plant and into the muslin. Carefully lift down the stems, shake them, and collect the seeds. Store in a paper bag.

FLOWERS

Lavender, fennel, chamomile, marigold, or borage flowers are easy to dry for future use.

1 Remove whole stems of flowers from the plant. Cut off the flowers with scissors making sure that no stem is left attached.

2 Scatter on muslin stretched over a frame. Leave in a dry, airy place out of direct sunlight for 3 weeks until brittle. Store in a sealed jar and use within 6 months.

CHILLIES

Dried chillies really hold their heat and flavour. Choose ripe blemish-free chillies for drying.

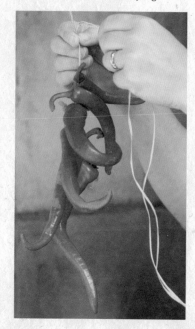

1 Thread a long piece of string through a very large needle. Pierce each chilli through the stalk and thread each chilli onto the string, leaving an extra length of string for hanging. Knot the bottom chilli in place.

2 Hang the string of chillies in an airy room away from direct sunlight to dry. Use within 8 months for the best flavour.

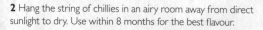

HOW TO PLAIT GARLIC

Garlic stalks must be dried before they can be plaited. Harvest the bulbs in early summer before the outer leaves start to decay. Keep their long stalks intact but do not let them dry so much that they become brittle. There should still be a little moisture at the centre of the stem.

1 Spread the bulbs out on a flat surface in a dry, airy, sheltered place out of direct sunlight for 2–4 weeks.

2 Give the bulbs a light brush to remove excess soil and then trim off the dried roots.

3 Nestle 3 bulbs together. Secure them with kitchen string if you like to hold them in place.

4 Repeat the 3-bulb pattern by setting a bulb straight on top and criss-crossing 2 more over that.

5 Divide the stems into 3 strands of 2 stalks each to plait. Bring the 2 right-hand stems up over to the left.

6 Repeat, crossing to the right using the central stem. Repeat a few more times and tie off in a knot at the end.

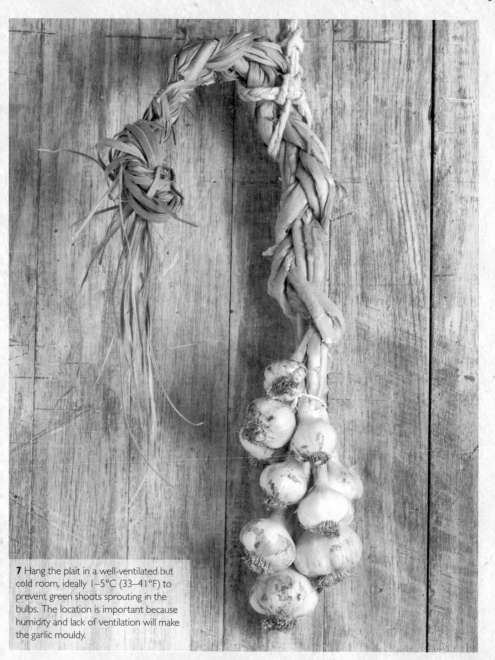

7 Hang the plait in a well-ventilated but cold room, ideally 1–5°C (33–41°F) to prevent green shoots sprouting in the bulbs. The location is important because humidity and lack of ventilation will make the garlic mouldy.

COOK

You've transformed your garden, now
do the same to your food. Perk up salads,
spice up salsas, and pack a punch with
marinades and sauces; knowing how to
use home-grown herbs will guarantee
flavoursome food.

PREPARATION

After harvesting your herbs wash, rinse, and dry them thoroughly. With most herbs the leaves must be separated from the stalks. Different herbs need different handling but tough stalks always need to be discarded.

STRIPPING
For preparing herbs with tough stalks.

Hold one end of the stalk with both hands. Move the thumb and first finger of one hand down the stalk pinching firmly to strip off the leaves.

PICKING
For preparing watercress leaves.

Separate watercress leaves and florets from the thick stalks. Discard the stalks and drop the leaves into ice-cold water to keep them fresh. Drain before using.

PLUCKING
For preparing herbs with tender stalks.

Hold the bottom of the stalk in one hand and pull the fronds up and outwards. Pluck the fronds from any remaining smaller stalks afterwards.

SLICING
For roughly chopping leaves and fronds.

Using a large chef's knife, slice up and down with one hand while guiding the herbs with the other, fingertips folded back so only knuckles are near the knife.

CHOPPING

Finely chopped herbs blend quickly into dressings, soups, and sauces. Coarsely chopped herbs keep their distinctive flavour and work well in slow cooking. Always rinse and dry herbs before chopping. Use a very sharp chef's knife or, for large amounts, use a mezzaluna or food processor.

Grasp the handle of a large chef's knife. Hold the point of the blade with the fingers of your other hand. Chop by rocking the knife up and down in the herbs.

Hold a handle of the mezzaluna in each hand. Chop in a side-to-side rocking motion. Heap the herbs back into a pile from time to time with the blade.

PILING

To save time, herbs with wide flat leaves, such as basil, sorrel, or mint, can be piled up and sliced.

1 Gently stack the leaves underside-up. The more leaves you include in a stack, the less slicing you will need to do. Try not to bruise the herbs as you handle them.

2 Hold the stack firmly and slice with a large chef's knife into thin shreds, keeping your fingertips well away from the blade.

SNIPPING SMALL LEAVES

Small-leaved herbs, such as curly or flatleaf parsley, chervil, fennel fronds, coriander, or tarragon, can be conveniently snipped in a wide bowl using a pair of sharp kitchen scissors.

Wash and thoroughly dry the herbs. Strip, pluck, or pick the leaves and discard the stems. Place the leaves in a wide bowl. Support the bowl with one hand and snip the herbs with the scissors, working your way round the bowl.

ROLLING AND SNIPPING LARGE LEAVES

Herbs with larger leaves, such as basil, sorrel, or mint, are easy to prepare by rolling them up and then snipping them with kitchen scissors. Be careful not to bruise the herbs as you handle them.

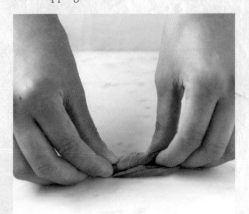

1 Gently stack a few large flat leaves, such as basil, sorrel, or mint, on top of one another underside-up. Roll them up securely into a cigar shape.

2 Hold the rolled herbs in one hand but keep your fingers back from the scissor blades. Snip through the pile into thin shreds.

SMASHING
For extracting the flavour of garlic cloves.

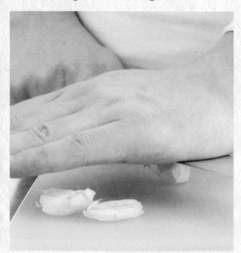

Put a few cloves on a cutting board. Lay the blade flat on top of a clove, and press down quickly and firmly with the palm of your hand.

BRUISING
For releasing essential oils in lemongrass.

Put the trimmed lemongrass on a cutting board. Lay the blade flat on top and press down firmly with your palm. This method also works with bay leaves and citrus peel.

POUNDING
A pestle and mortar is the best way to pound and mash herbs and seeds to release their flavours.

1 Put coarsely chopped or snipped herbs and seeds into the mortar. Pound straight down with the pestle until the herbs and seeds are smashed.

2 Beat the smashed mixture in a circular motion, mashing until you have a coarse purée. A pinch of sea salt and a tablespoon of olive oil helps the process.

PREPARING CHILLIES

Deseed your chillies before chopping them if you do not like them fiercely hot. Chopped chillies can then be placed in small freezer bags and frozen for up to 6 months.

I Lay the chilli on a cutting board. Using a sharp chef's knife, chop off the stalk and discard. Slice down the middle. Scrape out the seeds and discard.

2 Slice the chilli flesh lengthways into thin strips, skin-side down. Be sure to keep your fingertips away from the cutting edge of the knife.

3 Turn the strips over and slice across the width until they are very finely chopped. Take care never to touch your face or eyes when working with chillies and wash your hands thoroughly afterwards, or wear disposable plastic or latex gloves.

Chillies *The heat level of chillies can range from mild to blisteringly hot.*

GRATING

To get the most flavour from roots, such as horseradish or ginger, simply peel and grate them.

Slice off a chunk of fresh horseradish and peel the skin. Finely grate the amount of horseradish you need. Peeled roots can be frozen in a freezer bag and grated directly from the freezer. Reseal and return to the freezer immediately after use. Frozen horseradish and ginger will keep in the freezer for up to 6 months.

FLAVOURINGS

For tough, fibrous herbs, such as rosemary, thyme, and bay, it's a good idea to remove the herbs before serving after their flavours have infused into your cooking. You can brush ingredients with herbs, mix herbs in a bouquet garni, or put herbs, seeds, and peels in a muslin pouch.

BOUQUETS GARNIS

A staple in French cooking, these aromatic bunches of herbs enhance the flavour of slow-cooked dishes. Add them to a stew or pot roast before cooking, and discard before serving.

Herb brush *Dip a few herb sprigs in olive oil and brush roasts during cooking. Discard after use.*

For stronger flavours, make a large bouquet garni, using a generous handful of each of the herbs

Fresh bay leaf holds the bundle together and adds flavour

Leave enough string to tie a loop to hang over the pan so you can remove the bouquet garni easily after cooking

Wrap the string several times around the bunch and make a secure knot

MUSLIN POUCHES

Just like a bouquet garni in a bag, you can fill a muslin pouch with fresh or dried herbs.

1 Cut a piece of clean muslin into a square measuring 10 × 10cm (4 × 4in).

2 Place your selection of aromatic flavourings in the middle of the muslin square. Use more herbs for a stronger flavour.

3 Bring up the corners of the muslin to enclose the flavourings and tie them securely with a piece of kitchen string. Leave enough string to retrieve the pouch.

BEST COMBINATIONS

Lots of herbs complement each other when used together for flavouring particular ingredients. Here are some reliable combinations:

Classic Meat Parsley, thyme, and bay

Fish Parsley, thyme, lemon peel, and dill or fennel

Poultry Parsley, tarragon, thyme, and orange peel

Vegetables Sage, parsley, and marjoram or oregano

THE RECIPES

All your efforts in the garden, on the balcony, or on the window ledge have paid off and now it is time to get cooking. Fresh herbs shine in so many main and side dishes, such as soups, sauces, and salsas, and they enliven other ingredients in marinades, rubs, and coatings. The marinade, rub, and coating recipes do not feature cooking times – the way you cook your poultry, meat, or fish is entirely up to you.

BUTTERS

Simple combinations of chopped herbs and soft butter are an easy and versatile way to add a fresh aromatic touch to grilled or fried meats. To store butters, shape into a sausage, wrap in cling film, and twist the ends to seal. Keep in the fridge for up to 1 week or in the freezer for up to 3 months. To use, cut off discs as needed straight from the fridge or freezer.

WATERCRESS BUTTER

Peppery watercress and butter are a mouthwatering mix for grilled meats and fish. This butter can also be used as a sandwich spread.

MAKES 200G (7OZ) **PREP** 20 MINS

100g (3½oz) watercress, rinsed and dried
sea salt and freshly ground black pepper

100g (3½oz) unsalted butter, softened
    and cut into 10–12 pieces
2 tsp lemon juice

1 Tip the watercress into a colander, pick the leaves, and discard the stalks (see p122).
2 Put the leaves in the small bowl of a food processor in batches. Season with a little salt and more generously with pepper. Pulse quickly until finely chopped.
3 Add the butter to the watercress, and drizzle in the lemon juice. Whiz until smooth, or beat with a wooden spoon, and transfer to a small dish. Cover and chill until ready to use.

OREGANO BUTTER

Use to add an evocative Mediterranean touch to roasted vegetables and bruschetta.

MAKES 100G (3½OZ) **PREP** 20 MINS

1 scant tbsp groundnut or mild olive oil
100g (3½oz) unsalted butter, softened and cut
3 tbsp oregano, finely chopped

garlic clove
sea salt and freshly ground black pepper

1 Place a layer of kitchen paper on a plate. Put the oil and 2 tsp of the butter in a small non-stick frying pan over a medium heat. Add the oregano and garlic and stir-fry for 2 minutes. Remove the oregano and garlic, and spread them over the plate.
2 Whiz together the rest of the butter and the drained oregano and garlic in a food processor, pestle and mortar, or in a bowl with a fork. Season lightly with salt and pepper.
3 Transfer to a small dish, cover, and chill until ready to use.

TARRAGON BUTTER

This butter, with its lemony herbal flavour, is excellent when served melted over white fish, such as sole, cod, hake, plaice, and pollock.

MAKES 100G (3½OZ) **PREP** 15 MINS

3 tbsp tarragon, finely chopped
sea salt and freshly ground black pepper

100g (3½oz) very soft unsalted butter
2 tsp lemon juice

1 Put the tarragon into a small bowl. Season lightly with salt and pepper, and add the butter and lemon juice.
2 Mash everything together until creamy. Transfer to a small dish and chill until ready to use.

Cook's note To make the butter very soft, dice it and then mash it in a bowl with a fork over medium-hot water, or soften in the microwave on low for 1 minute.

SNAIL BUTTER

Though this is the traditional butter to serve sizzling hot with snails, it is also delicious with chicken or fish.

MAKES 150G (5½OZ) **PREP** 15 MINS

125g (4½oz) very soft unsalted butter
2½ tbsp lemon juice
3 tbsp finely chopped flatleaf or curly parsley

4 garlic cloves
sea salt and freshly ground black pepper

1 Mash together the butter and lemon juice until well mixed and creamy.
2 Beat in the parsley. Smash the garlic cloves with the flat of a knife, peel, sprinkle with salt, and crush in a pestle and mortar. Beat into the butter. Transfer to a small dish, cover, and chill for up to 3 days until ready to use. Do not freeze.

MONTPELLIER BUTTER

A pungent butter with a mild Tabasco kick. Serve it with grilled meat or fish.

MAKES 200G (7OZ) **PREP** 30 MINS

2 shallots, chopped
1 tbsp each chopped flatleaf (or curly) parsley, sorrel, coriander (or chervil), tarragon, chives, and spinach (or watercress)
2 cured anchovy fillets, drained of oil and chopped
2 small gherkins, chopped
1 tbsp capers, drained

1 garlic clove, smashed, peeled, and crushed
125g (4½oz) very soft unsalted butter
3 tbsp olive oil
sea salt and freshly ground black pepper
2 tsp white wine vinegar or tarragon vinegar (see p135)
a few drops Tabasco (optional)

1 Bring a kettle to the boil. Put a small pan over a moderate heat. Add the shallots, pour in boiling water to cover, and add the chopped herbs. Blanch for a minute, tip into a sieve, drain, refresh with cold water, drain well, and pat with the palm of your hand to extract excess moisture.
2 Spread the herbs and shallots over a plate lined with a double layer of kitchen paper. Press dry with more kitchen paper.
3 Using a food processor equipped with a small bowl, whiz the herb and shallot mixture together with the anchovies, gherkins, capers, garlic, and butter. Season with salt and pepper, scrape the sides of the bowl with a spatula, and trickle in the olive oil with the motor running.
4 Taste and adjust the seasoning. Stir in the vinegar and Tabasco, if using.
5 Transfer to a small dish, cover, and chill for at least 1 hour or up to a week. Do not freeze.

OILS AND VINEGARS

Herb oils and vinegars are the best substitute for fresh herbs. Use impeccably clean sterilized bottles and good quality oil or vinegar. Some oils are simply made by adding an ingredient, such as a chilli, to fruity olive oil.

ROSEMARY OIL

This oil is a kitchen treasure for drizzling over chicken and fish.

MAKES 250ML (8FL OZ) **PREP** 20 MINS **COOK** 15 MINS

2 garlic cloves, unpeeled
6 sprigs of rosemary, leaves only

250ml (8fl oz) fruity olive oil
3 small attractive sprigs of rosemary

1 Blanch the garlic for 3 minutes in a small pan of boiling water. Remove from the pan and refresh in cold water. Drain it, pat it dry, and peel.
2 Smash the rosemary leaves and garlic with the flat of a large kitchen knife (see p125). Put them into a small heavy pan, and pour in the oil. Bring to a simmer over a low heat, pushing down the leaves and garlic with a wooden spoon to extract their flavour. Cook and stir for 2–3 minutes. Take off the heat and leave until cold, still stirring and mashing occasionally.
3 Meanwhile, blanch the 3 rosemary sprigs for 2 minutes in boiling water. Refresh them in cold water, then drain and dry them.
4 Put the sprigs into a sterilized bottle (see p176). Line a funnel with dampened clean muslin, and place it in the neck of the bottle. Pour the oil slowly into the bottle. Seal and keep in a cool place. Use within 6 weeks.

TARRAGON VINEGAR

Use this vinegar in dressings or boil it up with diced shallot for a sauce.

MAKES 500ML (16FL OZ) **PREP** 20 MINS **INFUSE** 72 HOURS

500ml (16fl oz) white wine or cider vinegar
5 sprigs tarragon, plus 2–3 sprigs to finish

garlic clove
6 peppercorns

1 In a sterilized jar (see p176) combine the vinegar with the 5 sprigs of tarragon, garlic, and peppercorns. Cover, shake well, and leave to infuse for at least 24 hours or until the tarragon discolours, shaking from time to time.
2 Put 2 or 3 fresh tarragon sprigs in a new sterilized bottle. Strain the infused vinegar through a muslin-lined sieve into a jug. Discard the flavourings. Pour the vinegar into the bottle and seal. Keep in a cool place. Use after 48 hours and within 2 months.

RUBS

A rub is a mixture of herbs patted onto a main ingredient just before cooking, enhancing the aromatic appeal of a range of dishes. Remember that cooking changes the flavour of herbs. When roasting, cover loosely with foil so the herbs do not dry out too much. For added flavour, add extra fresh herbs right at the end of cooking.

PARSLEY, TARRAGON, AND LEMON THYME RUB

This mix of herbs is perfect with roast chicken – try easing a little under the skin.

FOR 1 MEDIUM CHICKEN OR 2 POUSSINS **SERVES** 4 **PREP** 15 MINS

1 tbsp finely chopped flatleaf or curly parsley
2 tsp dried tarragon
2 stalks lemon thyme, leaves stripped, stems discarded
1 tsp finely grated lemon zest
1 tsp sea salt
¼ tsp freshly ground black pepper

Mix all the ingredients together in a cup. Scatter the mixture all over the chicken, patting it in gently. If roasting, sprinkle over fruity olive oil or dot with soft butter.

Variations To stuff the chicken, use the same herb mixture and no salt. Halve the quantities, add 1 heaped tbsp fresh bread crumbs, and stir into 200g (7oz) sausagemeat or 200g (7oz) finely chopped fresh figs or apricots. Stir in 1 egg and pack loosely. For a lighter option, mix 100g (3½oz) fromage frais with 2 tbsp olive oil and add to the mixture.

FENNEL AND THYME RUB

The lemon juice moistens the herbs in this rub. Use with sea bass or red mullet.

FOR 600G (1LB 5OZ) FILLET OR 900G (2LB) WHOLE FISH **SERVES** 4 **PREP** 15 MINS

½ tbsp finely chopped flatleaf or curly parsley
2 tsp dried fennel or dill seeds, crushed
2 stalks thyme, leaves stripped, stems discarded
1 tbsp lemon juice
¼ tsp freshly ground white pepper

Mix the herbs and seeds in a cup. Stir in the lemon juice and white pepper. Scatter all over the fish (the lemon juice helps them stick to the fish), and smooth in gently.

Cook's note For a whole fish, use the same herb mix to flavour the cavity. Put in a shallow bowl. Slice half a lemon, dip the slices in the mixture, and slip inside the cavity of the fish.

SAGE, JUNIPER, AND BAY LEAF RUB

Aromatic juniper, sage, and bay leaf work well with strongly flavoured game and pork.

FOR 800G (1¾LB) MEAT **SERVES** 4 **PREP** 15 MINS

I tbsp dried sage, crushed
I tsp juniper berries
2 bay leaves, finely snipped
2 stalks thyme
I tsp salt

I garlic clove, crushed
I tsp finely grated orange zest
I tsp coarsely ground black pepper
150g (5½oz) mascarpone cheese (use
  this for pork roast only)

Mix all the ingredients together in a cup. (For pork roast, add the mascarpone cheese.) Scatter the mixture all over the meat and pat it in lightly. If roasting, sprinkle over fruity olive oil or dot with butter. Scatter over a few fresh bay leaves towards the end of cooking.

OREGANO, CITRUS, AND ROSEMARY RUB

Woody, citrussy flavours set off the sweet richness of lamb in this fragrant rub.

FOR 800G (1¾LB) LAMB **SERVES** 4 **PREP** 15 MINS

I tsp chopped oregano or ½ tsp dried oregano
2 tsp finely grated lemon zest
small garlic clove, crushed
½ tsp ground cumin

I tsp chopped rosemary leaves
I tbsp chopped coriander
sea salt and freshly ground black pepper

Mix all the ingredients together in a cup. Scatter all over the meat, patting it in gently. Just before cooking, season with salt and pepper. If roasting, sprinkle over fruity olive oil. Towards the end of cooking, sprinkle over 2 tbsp lemon juice and scatter over some chopped oregano.

PERSILLADE

Add persillade to slow-cooked dishes at the end of cooking to liven them up.

SERVES 4 **PREP** 10 MINS

3 tbsp finely chopped flatleaf or curly parsley
I or 2 garlic cloves, crushed
sea salt and freshly ground black pepper

Mix the parsley with the garlic. Season with salt and pepper and stir lightly into pot roasts, stews, and casseroles after you have taken the dish off the heat.

Variations For Italian gremolata, add 2 tsp finely grated citrus zest to the mixture. For a gratin dish, stir 3 tbsp fresh breadcrumbs into persillade or gremolata, sprinkle over the gratin, drizzle with olive oil or dot with butter. Continue baking for 10–15 minutes.

COATINGS

Halfway between simple dry rubs and wet marinades, coatings wrap meat and fish in an aromatic layer. Their flavours blend in with the ingredients as they cook and add a nice touch of texture to the dish.

SAGE AND PARSLEY COATING (PICTURED)

The highly fragrant herbs in this coating work wonders on poultry.

COATS I MEDIUM CHICKEN OR 2 POUSSINS **SERVES** 4 **PREP** 20 MINS **CHILL** 30 MINS

2 garlic cloves, smashed
sea salt
8 sage leaves, chopped
2 tbsp chopped flatleaf parsley
I tsp thyme

I tsp summer or winter savory, chopped
I tsp Szechuan peppercorns
40–50g (I ½oz) butter, very soft
2 tbsp mild olive oil

1 Place the garlic, a little sea salt, sage, and parsley into a mortar and mash.
2 Add the thyme, savory, and peppercorns and continue mashing together.
3 Add the butter and the oil. Pound down with the pestle a few times, and then mix the ingredients together using a circular movement.
4 Put the poultry in a dish. Spoon half of the mixture onto it. Smooth the paste over the whole surface and press down gently. Turn the poultry over, and repeat until coated.
5 Cover loosely with cling film and chill for at least 30 minutes.

CORIANDER AND MINT COATING

This robust paste gives shoulder of lamb a warm Mediterranean spiciness.

COATS 600G (ILB 5OZ) LAMB **SERVES** 4 **PREP** 15 MINS **CHILL** 30 MINS

2 garlic cloves, smashed and peeled
I tsp cumin seeds
½ tsp ground cumin
½ tsp ground coriander
I tbsp chopped fresh coriander

I tsp dried mint
I tsp finely grated lemon zest
3 tbsp fruity olive oil
2 tsp rosemary
sea salt and freshly ground black pepper

1 Whiz the garlic, cumin, coriander, mint, and lemon zest in a food processor using the pulse mode. Whiz in the olive oil. Stop the motor.
2 Stir the rosemary into the mixture, and season with pepper.
3 Put the lamb on a dish. Spoon half the mixture onto it. Smooth it over the whole surface and press down gently. Turn the lamb over, and repeat until coated.
4 Cover the lamb loosely with cling film and chill for at least 30 minutes. Season with salt before cooking.

HORSERADISH AND BAY LEAF COATING

All the classic combinations for beef – horseradish, bay leaves, mustard seeds, and peppercorns – are here, giving the coating lots of texture and a fiery kick.

COATS 600G (1LB 5OZ) BEEF **SERVES** 4 **PREP** 15 MINS **CHILL** 30 MINS

1 garlic clove	1 tbsp finely chopped flatleaf
1 tsp black peppercorns	or curly parsley
1 tsp mustard seeds	1 tbsp mild olive oil
2 tsp freshly grated horseradish	2 tbsp very soft butter
2 finely chopped bay leaves	sea salt

1 Use a pestle and mortar (or, if you prefer, whiz the ingredients quickly in a food processor using the pulse mode). Put the garlic and peppercorns in the bowl. Smash down with the pestle to crush. Add the mustard seeds and grated horseradish, bay leaves, and parsley. Pound down with the pestle until smashed and mixed.

2 Add the oil and butter, pound down a few times, then beat to mix using a circular movement (see p125).

3 Put the beef in the centre of a plate. Spoon half the mixture onto the centre of the beef. Spread the mixture outwards, smoothing it over the whole surface with your hands. Turn over, spoon the rest of the mixture over the beef, and smooth it down until the beef is completely coated.

4 Cover loosely with cling film and chill for at least 30 minutes to give the flavours time to release into the beef, or longer if you prefer more developed flavours (overnight is ideal). Season with salt just before cooking.

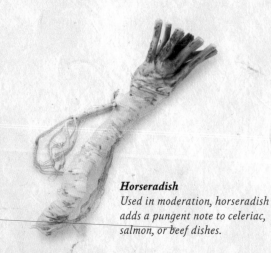

Horseradish
Used in moderation, horseradish adds a pungent note to celeriac, salmon, or beef dishes.

DILL AND CORIANDER COATING

This coating is for salmon, and gives it an attractive warm red-brown colour.

COATS 700G (1½LB) SALMON FILLET **SERVES** 4 **PREP** 15 MINS **CHILL** 15 MINS

2 tbsp chopped dill fronds
1 tbsp chopped coriander
1 tbsp chopped basil
½ tsp coarsely ground white pepper
1 tbsp soy sauce
1 tsp caster sugar or honey
¼ tsp hot paprika

1 tbsp mild olive oil, plus a little extra to finish
1 tbsp very soft butter, plus a little extra to finish
2 tsp finely chopped chives
1 tbsp lemon juice and 1 tsp finely grated zest
sea salt

1 Put the dill, coriander, basil, white pepper, soy sauce, sugar or honey, and paprika in the small bowl of a food processor. Whiz using the pulse mode. Whiz in the olive oil and butter and stop the motor.

2 Stir the chives and the lemon juice and zest into the mixture, and adjust the seasoning to taste.

3 Spoon half the mixture over the centre of the salmon fillet. Spread over the whole surface using the palms of your hands. Turn over, spoon the rest of the mixture over the salmon, and smooth down until completely coated.

4 Cover the salmon loosely with cling film. Chill for at least 15 minutes to give the flavours time to develop. Dot with a little extra butter or add a sprinkling of olive oil just before cooking.

Coriander
*Versatile coriander is the
traditional flavouring for fish
dishes in many parts of the world.*

MARINADES

The liquid in marinades, usually alcohol or citrus juice, tenderizes and part-cooks the meat. At the same time, the herbs impart their flavour. Be generous and add plenty of herbs to the infusion.

BAY LEAF, LOVAGE, AND JUNIPER MARINADE

This marinade brings out the very best in venison and beef. For tougher cuts and more mature meat, leave it to marinate for up to 48 hours.

COATS 1–1.5KG (2¼–3⅓LB) MEAT **SERVES** 4–6 **PREP** 15 MINS **COOK** 20 MINS **MARINATE** 4 HOURS

- 1 garlic clove
- 4 bay leaves
- 4–6 sprigs flatleaf parsley, both leaves and stalks, chopped
- 2 sprigs lovage, chopped
- 1 Welsh onion (or 2 spring onions), chopped
- 1 shallot, roughly chopped
- 6 juniper berries
- 12 black peppercorns
- 5cm (2in) piece dried orange peel
- 750ml (1¼ pints) smooth, mellow, good-quality red wine

1 Smash the garlic with the flat of a knife, then peel and crush in a pestle and mortar. Smash the bay leaves with a kitchen mallet. Put these in a medium pan and add the herbs and chopped onion and shallot. Add the juniper berries, peppercorns, and orange peel. Pour in the red wine and 250ml (8fl oz) water. Bring to the boil over a high heat.

2 Once it is boiling, reduce the heat and partially cover. Let it simmer for 5 minutes to allow the raw alcohol taste of the wine to disappear.

3 Take off the heat and leave to cool. Put the beef or venison in a slightly larger bowl or non-metallic container big enough to hold the meat and the marinade. Pour the marinade over the meat and turn it over a couple of times. Cover and refrigerate for at least 4 hours (ideally overnight) to give time for the flavours to infuse and the wine to tenderize the meat. Turn the meat 2–3 times during marinating.

4 When you are ready to cook the meat, remove the dish from the fridge. Lift out the meat and drain it well. If you intend to fry or roast the meat, pat it dry with kitchen paper. Push the marinade through a sieve into a jug. It will be highly aromatic and makes an ideal cooking liquid or base for stock or gravy.

CITRUS AND BASIL MARINADE

This marinade is for pork. As it roasts in the oven with the meat the marinade reduces to a thick syrupy sauce.

COATS 600G (1LB 5OZ) PORK TENDERLOIN **SERVES** 4 **PREP** 15 MINS **MARINATE** 1 HOUR

juice of 2 unwaxed oranges
finely grated zest of 1 unwaxed orange
3 tbsp soy sauce
12 sweet basil leaves, finely chopped
12–15 chives, finely chopped
3cm (1in) piece fresh root ginger, grated

2 garlic cloves
1 tsp coriander seeds
400ml (14fl oz) plain yoghurt
2 tbsp mild olive oil
sea salt and freshly ground black pepper

1 Put the orange juice and zest in a bowl large enough to hold the pork and the marinade. Stir in the soy sauce and add the basil, chives, and grated ginger.

2 Pound the garlic cloves and coriander seeds using a pestle and mortar or the flat side of a large knife (see p125) and add them to the bowl. Stir to mix. Then stir in the yoghurt and oil. Season with salt and pepper to taste.

3 Add the meat to the marinade. Using your hands or a spoon, turn the pork over several times until it is evenly coated. Cover the dish with cling film and leave in the fridge to marinate for at least 1 hour before cooking. Leave it to marinate longer if you prefer stronger flavours.

Variation This also tastes wonderful with chicken, and coats 4–6 leg or breast portions or 1 whole medium chicken.

Sweet basil
Eggs, poultry, pork,
peppers, and tomatoes
are all enhanced by basil.

NO-COOK MARINADES

Marinades can be used to cold-cook very fresh fish and vegetables. The process also develops and changes the flavours of the herbs. Add more fresh herbs just before serving to deepen the flavour.

DILLED SMOKED HADDOCK

Use fresh undyed smoked haddock fillet for this tangy appetizer.

SERVES 6 AS A STARTER PREP 15 MINS MARINATE 1–2 HOURS FINISH 10 MINS

1 tsp chopped dill fronds, plus 1½ tsp to finish
2 tsp finely chopped flatleaf or curly parsley
1 tsp finely chopped chives, plus 1 tsp to finish
1 tsp finely chopped stripped thyme leaves
juice and finely grated zest of 1 small lemon
1 tbsp fruity olive oil, plus 3 tbsp to finish
400g (14oz) smoked haddock fillet

To serve
1 lemon, cut into wedges
6 slices toasted bread
1 garlic clove, peeled and halved
butter for spreading

1 Put the herbs in a shallow bowl. Add the lemon juice and zest, and 1 tbsp of the olive oil. Stir well and set aside while you prepare the fish.
2 Wipe the fish clean. Remove any remaining bones. Shred with a fork. Add to the herb marinade and stir to coat. Cover and chill for 1–2 hours.
3 Transfer the fish to a large sieve, and drain well. Pat gently dry with kitchen paper (don't worry if some of the herbs come off). Transfer to a serving bowl, sprinkle over the 3 tbsp olive oil and the reserved herbs. Toss gently. Serve at once with lemon wedges and toast rubbed with the cut sides of a garlic clove and lightly buttered.

CUCUMBER WITH TARRAGON AND CREAM

Tarragon's aniseed flavour is perfect with marinated cucumber and cream.

SERVES 4 AS A STARTER PREP 15 MINS STAND 30 MINS FINISH 10 MINS

1 large firm unblemished cucumber, peeled and
  thinly sliced
2 tbsp coarse sea salt
½ tsp caster sugar

1 tbsp chopped tarragon, plus 2 tsp to
  finish
4 tbsp single cream, or 3 tbsp soured cream
freshly ground black pepper

1 Put the cucumber in a colander. Mix the salt, sugar, and tarragon, and sprinkle over the cucumber. Toss, then put a weighted plate on top. Leave for 30 minutes.
2 Rinse in plenty of cold water to get rid of any excess salt, drain well, and press down hard to extract all the moisture. Pat dry with kitchen paper.
3 Transfer to a serving bowl. Spoon over the cream, toss lightly, and scatter over the reserved tarragon. Stir lightly, season with pepper, and serve. This dish can be refrigerated overnight.

COURGETTE WITH CHIVE MARINADE

Chive and thyme flavour the courgettes while the marinade draws out their excess moisture to create a flavourful and succulent dish.

SERVES 4 AS A STARTER **PREP** 20 MINS **STAND** 40 MINS **FINISH** 10 MINS

400g (14oz) small firm unblemished courgettes
4 tbsp fruity olive oil
2 tbsp lemon juice and 1 tbsp finely grated zest
1 tsp finely chopped chives, plus 2 tsp to finish
1 tsp finely chopped flatleaf or curly parsley plus 1 tsp to finish
1 tsp finely chopped thyme
sea salt and freshly ground black pepper

1 Rinse the courgettes, pat them dry, and then top and tail them. Using a vegetable peeler, shave lengthways into thin strips (it doesn't matter if some strips are just peel or a little thicker). Reserve on a plate lined with a double layer of kitchen paper.
2 In a bowl, mix 1 tbsp of the olive oil with the lemon juice and zest, chives, parsley, and thyme, and season lightly with salt and pepper. Add the courgette strips and toss to coat. Leave to stand in a cool place for at least 40 minutes.
3 Tip into a colander. Drain well, pressing down gently, then pat dry with kitchen paper.
4 Transfer to a serving bowl. Spoon over the reserved olive oil, chives, and parsley, and toss lightly. Taste and season with salt and pepper. Serve at room temperature.

MUSHROOMS À LA GRECQUE

Chervil and coriander add a fresh herb flavour to this popular starter.

SERVES 4–6 AS A STARTER **PREP** 20 MINS **MARINATE** 4 HOURS **FINISH** 10 MINS

4 tbsp fruity olive oil, plus 2 tbsp to finish
1 garlic clove, smashed, peeled, and crushed
3 tbsp lemon juice and 2 tsp finely grated zest
2 tbsp finely chopped flatleaf parsley
1 tsp crushed coriander seeds
1 tbsp chopped chervil, plus 1 tbsp to finish
400g (14oz) very fresh white round cap mushrooms, wiped clean with damp kitchen paper and thinly sliced
sea salt and freshly ground black pepper
1 tbsp chopped coriander
2 tsp sherry vinegar

1 In a bowl, combine the olive oil, crushed garlic, lemon juice and zest, parsley, coriander seeds, and chervil.
2 Add the sliced mushrooms to the bowl and season lightly with salt and pepper. Toss, cover, and leave to marinate in the fridge for 4 hours.
3 Tip into a colander, and drain off any excess liquid. Stir in the extra 2 tbsp of olive oil and the vinegar, and season. Scatter over the reserved chervil and the chopped coriander. Serve soon at room temperature.

SALSAS

Nothing awakens the taste buds like a salsa, whether it is hot and fiery or luxuriously creamy and cooling. Use salsas for dipping or pouring, with grilled seafood, poultry, or pork, or with raw vegetables.

LEMONGRASS AND CHILLI SALSA

This salsa transforms grilled fish or skewers of barbecued white meat.

SERVES 6 **PREP** 20 MINS **CHILL** I HOUR

2 stalks lemongrass, outer leaves discarded
2 heaped tbsp chopped Thai basil,
  plus 6 extra leaves to finish
I tsp freshly grated root ginger
I whole red chilli, seeded and finely chopped

I tbsp runny honey or I tbsp sugar
3 tbsp soy sauce
2 tsp fish sauce
6 tbsp lime juice

I Slice off the tops of the lemongrass stalks and discard them. Bash down on the bulb ends with the side of a large knife or pound using a kitchen mallet (see p125). Chop very finely and place in a bowl.
2 Add the basil, the ginger, and the chilli.
3 Pour in the honey or sugar, the soy sauce, fish sauce, and the lime juice, and stir well. Cover and chill for at least 1 hour to give the flavours time to develop.
4 Just before serving stir in the reserved whole basil leaves.

Chilli
A touch of chilli adds a magic heat to salsas and curries and brings out the flavours of other herbs and spices.

AVOCADO, PAPRIKA, AND LIME SALSA

Nutty avocado with a hint of spice and citrus make a good side dish for hot curries and grilled fish or poultry.

SERVES 4–6 **PREP** 20 MINS **CHILL** 30 MINS

2 ripe vine tomatoes
2 ripe Hass avocados, halved, pitted, and peeled
juice of 1 lime
4–5 sprigs coriander

3–4 sprigs flatleaf parsley
sea salt and freshly ground black pepper
¼ tsp hot paprika
1 tbsp mild olive oil

1 Place the tomatoes into boiling water for 1 minute. Lift them out with a large spoon and when they are cool enough to handle, peel and halve them. Scoop out and discard the seeds, remove the tomato core, and cut into small dice. Set aside.
2 Cut the avocado flesh into small dice about the same size as the diced tomatoes. Put in a bowl, pour over the lime juice, and toss gently. Add the herbs, season with salt and pepper, and then add the paprika.
3 Stir the diced tomatoes into the mixture. Chill for 30 minutes or until ready to use. Stir through the olive oil, and season before serving.

ROCKET AND MASCARPONE SALSA

This is a tasty dip for garlicky toast, crudité batons, and steamed new potatoes.

SERVES 4–6 **PREP** 20 MINS **CHILL** 30 MINS

50g (1¾oz) rocket
2 tbsp roughly chopped chives
2 tbsp chervil
sea salt and freshly ground black pepper

100g (3½oz) mascarpone
100g (3½oz) ricotta
1 tbsp balsamic vinegar

1 Put the rocket, half the chives, and half the chervil in the small bowl of a food processor and season lightly with salt and pepper. Pulse briefly. Add the mascarpone and ricotta. Pulse again to mix but do not overprocess.
2 Transfer to a bowl, cover, and chill for 30 minutes or until ready to use. Stir in the balsamic vinegar, adjust the seasoning, and add the remaining chives and chervil.

DILL, WATERCRESS, CAPER, AND TOMATO SALSA

Fresh and citrussy, this salsa is fabulous with grilled white fish or prawns.

SERVES 4–6 **PREP** 15 MINS **CHILL** 30 MINS

2 tbsp chopped dill fronds
50g (1¾oz) picked watercress leaves, chopped
9 baby cherry tomatoes, halved
1 heaped tbsp capers, drained

juice and finely grated zest of ½ lemon
sea salt and freshly ground black pepper
3 tbsp fruity olive oil

1 Put the dill and watercress in a bowl. Gently squeeze the halved cherry tomatoes to discard some of the seeds, slice them again to quarter them, and add them to the bowl. Stir in the capers (if they are large, chop them first) and lemon juice and zest. Chill for 30 minutes or until ready to use.
2 Stir, season with salt and pepper, and drizzle with olive oil. Stir again before serving.

Variation For a chilli, coriander, and red onion salsa, use the same method but replace the dill with 2 tbsp chopped coriander. Replace the tomatoes with 1 small finely chopped red onion and, instead of using the capers, add 1 heaped tbsp chopped fresh walnut halves or pecan kernels. Drizzle with 1½ tbsp olive oil and 1½ tbsp walnut oil.

Dill
*Dill fronds give a lovely
parsley-aniseed flavour to a
wide range of dishes.*

SALADS

Fresh herbs and flowers add zing, excitement, and texture to everyday salad ingredients. Be creative, and use whatever is in season, and remember – the fresher the better. Tear everything into bite-sized pieces.

DANDELION, ROCKET, AND FLOWER SALAD

Dress this exuberant pretty salad at the last minute and as lightly as possible.

SERVES 4 **PREP** 15 MINS

For the dressing
4 tbsp groundnut, sunflower, or grapeseed oil, plus 1 tbsp to finish
sea salt and freshly ground black pepper
1 tbsp tarragon or white wine vinegar
½ tsp caster sugar
4 lovage leaves, finely chopped

For the salad
125g (4½oz) lightly packed young tender dandelion greens, rinsed and dried
80–90g (3oz) rocket, loosely torn
80–90g (3oz) pea shoots, loosely torn
2 tbsp chopped flatleaf parsley
2 tbsp chopped chervil
1 tbsp small mint leaves
1 tbsp finely chopped chives
½ cup edible flowers, such as nasturtium or chive flowers, or sweet violet or pansy flower petals

1 Select a wide shallow salad bowl and prepare the dressing. Pour in the oil and season with salt and pepper. Whisk in the vinegar and sugar, and stir in the lovage.
2 Loosely tear up half the dandelion greens, and drop them into the bowl. Scatter half the rocket and half the pea shoots over the dandelion greens. Then add half the parsley, chervil, and mint. Do not toss.
3 Scatter over the remaining leaves, still without tossing.
4 Just before serving, scatter in the chives and flowers. Sprinkle over the reserved 1 tbsp of oil and season lightly.
5 Toss gently to coat the leaves, herbs, and flowers. Serve as soon as possible.

Dandelion
With its slightly bitter flavour, raw dandelion is best added in moderation.

HERB TABBOULEH

Here is an intensively herby version of tabbouleh, a Middle Eastern classic.

SERVES 4 **PREP** 25 MINS

For the dressing

1 garlic clove, smashed, peeled, and crushed
sea salt and freshly ground black pepper
½ tsp five-spice powder
1 tbsp lemon juice and 1 tsp finely grated
  unwaxed lemon zest
1 tbsp pomegranate molasses or balsamic
  vinegar
4 tbsp fruity olive oil

For the salad

75g (2½oz) fine bulghur wheat
6 tbsp chopped flatleaf parsley
1 tbsp finely chopped mint
1 tbsp chopped coriander
4 spring onions, finely chopped
4 baby cherry tomatoes, chopped

1 Make the dressing in the bottom of a salad bowl. Mix the garlic with a little salt, the five-spice powder, lemon juice and zest, and the pomegranate molasses or balsamic vinegar. Whisk in the olive oil and season with salt and pepper to taste. Leave to stand while you prepare the ingredients for the salad.

2 Put the bulghur in a shallow bowl, cover with piping hot water, and leave to swell for 2 minutes. Tip into a sieve, drain, and refresh with plenty of cold water, rubbing the bulghur grains between your fingers. Shake the bulghur and then drain it well.

3 Tip the bulghur into the bowl with the dressing mixture. Add the parsley, mint, coriander, spring onions, and tomatoes. Toss just before serving and season with salt and pepper.

Variation You can add 2 or 3 tbsp pomegranate seeds for a crunchy jewel-like finish.

Flatleaf parsley
A true kitchen essential, flatleaf parsley
can be trusted to improve the flavour of
practically any savoury dish.

SHEPHERD'S SALAD

Also called Arabic salad, this is a popular dish in Turkey and the Middle East.

SERVES 4 **PREP** 20 MINS

For the dressing
½ garlic clove, crushed
½ tsp sweet paprika
½ tsp ground sumac
½ tsp caster sugar
½ tsp ground cumin
2 tbsp lemon juice and 1 tsp finely grated
   unwaxed lemon zest
7 tbsp fruity olive oil
sea salt and freshly ground black pepper

For the salad
1 large cucumber, peeled
15 baby cherry tomatoes
1 head sweet romaine or soft lettuce
12 black olives, pitted and chopped
3 spring onions, chopped
2 tbsp chopped flatleaf parsley
2 tbsp chopped purslane or rocket
2 tbsp chopped coriander
2 tbsp chopped mint

1 Make the dressing in the bottom of a salad bowl. Mix all the ingredients for the dressing and season with salt and pepper to taste. Leave the mixture to rest while you prepare the salad ingredients.

2 Cut the cucumber into 4 segments lengthways, scoop out the seeds, and discard them. Cut the flesh into small neat chunks. Reserve on a plate. Halve the tomatoes, scoop out and discard some of the seeds, and add to the cucumber. Tear or chop the lettuce into bite-sized pieces.

3 Stir the dressing. Put a layer of lettuce in the bowl (do not toss), scatter in some olives and spring onion, and sprinkle in some parsley, purslane or wild rocket, coriander, and mint. Add half the cucumber and tomatoes. Continue adding the ingredients until everything is in the bowl.

4 Toss the salad just before serving.

Variation For a spring herb salad with goat's cheese, omit the paprika, sumac, caster sugar, and cumin. Place half the amount of the olive oil, garlic, and lemon in a shallow bowl and mix. Top with 4 heaped tbsp each of freshly picked chervil, flatleaf parsley, chopped spring onions, and 2 tbsp each of lemon balm, chives, and dill fronds, all chopped. Scatter over 4 tbsp of crumbled fresh goat's cheese. Toss at the last minute just before serving.

SALAD WITH CHERVIL AND GREEN BEANS

Full of aromatic flavours and bursting with colour, this salad makes a good light lunch or substantial starter.

SERVES 4 **PREP** 30 MINS **COOK** 10 MINS

400g (14oz) green beans, topped and tailed
sea salt and freshly ground black pepper
3 tbsp finely chopped curly parsley
2 tsp lemon thyme
1 tbsp chopped fennel fronds
2 tbsp fruity olive oil
125g (4½oz) rocket (or watercress)
400g (14oz) can artichoke hearts, drained
    and halved
4 slices Parma ham, torn into thin shreds

16 small black olives, pitted and chopped
125g (4½oz) cherry tomatoes, halved
2 spring onions, chopped
3 tbsp chopped chervil

For the dressing
5 tbsp fruity olive oil
sea salt and freshly ground black pepper
½ garlic clove, crushed
1½ tbsp balsamic vinegar

1 Bring a pan of lightly salted water to the boil. Add the green beans and blanch for 5–7 minutes. Refresh in cold water, and drain.

2 Place the beans in a wide shallow salad bowl. Season them lightly with salt and pepper and scatter over half the parsley, lemon thyme, and fennel. Drizzle over the olive oil, toss, and set aside.

3 Make the dressing by pouring the olive oil into a small jug. Season with salt and pepper and then whisk in the garlic and the balsamic vinegar.

4 Scatter half the rocket over the beans, then half the artichoke hearts, ham, olives, tomatoes, and spring onion. Whisk the dressing and dribble half of it over the salad. Toss gently. Add the other half of the remaining salad ingredients, except the chervil.

5 Pour on the remaining dressing. Toss, sprinkle over the chervil, and serve.

Chervil
This delicate herb is perfect
for salads and egg dishes. Its
flavour vanishes if overcooked.

DRESSINGS AND VINAIGRETTES

Traditionally used to coat leaf salads, herby dressings are also excellent with plainly grilled fish or meats, and cooked vegetables or pulses. Mix the dressing slightly ahead of serving, but do not toss or drizzle over until the last minute.

CHILLI, CHIVE, AND GARLIC DRESSING

Try this Thai-style dressing with prawns, chicken, or steamed vegetables.

SERVES 4 **PREP** 10 MINS

1 tbsp chopped chives	1 tsp fish sauce
1 small garlic clove, crushed	2 tbsp lime juice
½ small red chilli, deseeded and chopped	1 tsp caster sugar
1 tbsp chopped coriander	60ml (2fl oz) groundnut oil

1 Put the chives, garlic, chilli, coriander, fish sauce, lime juice, and caster sugar in the small bowl of a food processor. Pulse to combine.
2 With the motor running, trickle in the groundnut oil, whizzing briefly until smooth. Serve soon or cover with cling film and refrigerate for up to 24 hours until ready to use. Stir before using.

MINT DRESSING

This fresh citrussy vinaigrette is wonderful on grilled lamb chops.

SERVES 4 **PREP** 10 MINS

4 tbsp chopped mint	1 tbsp lime juice
75ml (2½fl oz) fruity olive oil	1 tsp fish sauce
1 tbsp freshly squeezed orange juice	1 tsp caster sugar

1 Put the mint in the small bowl of a food processor, and pulse to purée.
2 Add the olive oil, orange and lime juices, fish sauce, and caster sugar. Whiz briefly until smooth. Serve soon or cover and refrigerate for up to 24 hours until ready to use. Stir before serving.

PARSLEY, CAPER, AND OLIVE VINAIGRETTE

Use this tangy vinaigrette on coleslaw, grilled or barbecued lamb, or prawns.

SERVES 4 **PREP** 10 MINS

I heaped tbsp chopped flatleaf parsley	¼ tsp Dijon mustard
½ small garlic clove, smashed, peeled, and crushed	½ tbsp chopped black olives
I tsp dried oregano	I tsp capers, drained
¼ tsp caster sugar	I½ tbsp balsamic vinegar
	60ml (2fl oz) fruity olive oil

1 Put the parsley, garlic, oregano, sugar, mustard, olives, capers, and balsamic vinegar in the small bowl of a food processor, and pulse to combine.
2 With the motor running, trickle in the olive oil, whizzing briefly until well mixed. Serve soon or cover and refrigerate for up to 24 hours until ready to use. If you find the sauce is a little too thick you can thin it down slightly by stirring in a splash of water. Stir well before using.

WARM TOMATO AND GARLIC VINAIGRETTE

Dress grilled tuna, poached fish, boiled chicken, or rice with this vinaigrette.

SERVES 4–6 **PREP** 10 MINS **COOK** 10 MINS

3 ripe medium-large vine tomatoes	I tbsp finely chopped basil
45ml (1½fl oz) olive oil	I tbsp finely chopped flatleaf parsley
2 garlic cloves, smashed, peeled, and crushed	I tbsp sherry vinegar
¼ tsp hot paprika	sea salt and freshly ground black pepper

1 Place the tomatoes in a bowl, cover them with boiling water, and leave for 1 minute. When they are cool enough to handle, peel. Halve them and then scoop out and discard the seeds. Remove the tomato core, cut the flesh into dice, and set aside.
2 Put the olive oil in a pan over a very low heat, and add the garlic and paprika. Stir for 3–4 minutes. Add half the basil and parsley, and stir for a minute. Add the tomatoes and stir gently for 2–3 minutes until hot.
3 Take off the heat. Stir in the reserved basil and parsley and then the sherry vinegar. Season with salt and pepper to taste and serve while still warm.

PESTO

The famous Genoese pesto is traditionally made by patiently pounding basil and garlic with a pestle and mortar until they become a coarse scented purée into which you beat olive oil, pine nuts, and Parmesan cheese. You can make pestos with other fresh herbs, such as parsley and coriander, and you can replace the pine nuts with fresh skinned walnuts.

MIXED HERB PESTO

Oregano gives a nice kick to this pesto. Toss it with pasta or stir it into rice.

SERVES 2 **PREP** 15 MINS **COOK** 20 MINS

3 tbsp coarsely chopped basil
2 tsp coarsely chopped oregano
3 tbsp coarsely chopped flatleaf parsley
2 garlic cloves
coarse sea salt

50g (1¾oz) Parmesan cheese, grated
90–100ml (3–3½fl oz) fruity olive oil
freshly ground black pepper
300g (10oz) dried pasta
1 tbsp single cream (optional)

1 Put the herbs in a large mortar, reserving 1 tbsp to finish. Smash the garlic with the flat of a knife (see p125), peel, and add to the mortar. Sprinkle in a little salt. Pound down onto the mixture with the pestle until it is mushy.

2 Add the Parmesan a little at a time and beat vigorously to blend. Slowly beat in the olive oil until you have a thick coarse paste, and season with salt and pepper to taste.

3 Cook the pasta according to the pack instructions. Drain, reserving 2 tbsp of the cooking water. Stir the water into the pesto to loosen it slightly. Return the pasta to the hot pan and tip in the pesto. Toss to coat thoroughly. Stir in the reserved fresh herbs. If using the cream, stir it in and serve immediately.

Cook's note To use some of the pesto as a salad dressing, after step 3, whisk in a little balsamic or other vinegar or lemon juice. To dress a salad for 4, use 3–4 tbsp pesto and 1 tbsp balsamic vinegar.

Oregano
Fresh or dried, this wonderful herb is
a classic ingredient in many popular
vegetable and shellfish dishes.

COLD SAUCES

Herbs play an essential part in flavouring cold sauces where they also help counteract fatty oil or heavy cream. Fresh herbs work the best, but dried herbs, such as mint, oregano, thyme, and marjoram, can be used ground and in small amounts.

SAUCE VERTE

This Mediterranean favourite is particularly good with poached chicken or salmon, and with grilled tuna.

MAKES 250ML (8FL OZ) **PREP** 20 MINS

- 1 tbsp fresh breadcrumbs made from day-old bread
- 1 tbsp white wine vinegar
- 1 tsp Dijon mustard
- 175ml (6fl oz) fruity olive oil
- 5 tbsp finely chopped flatleaf or curly parsley, plus stalks (optional)
- 3 tbsp finely chopped basil
- 1 tbsp finely chopped mint
- 2 garlic cloves, crushed
- 2 anchovy fillets, chopped
- 2 tbsp capers, drained, and finely chopped
- 2–3 tbsp lemon juice and 2 tsp finely grated unwaxed lemon zest
- sea salt and freshly ground black pepper

1 In a bowl, mix the breadcrumbs and vinegar together with the mustard and 3 tbsp of the olive oil.

2 Add the herbs (reserving 1 heaped tbsp of the mixed herbs to finish), and beat well. If you like, chop a few parsley stalks very finely and stir them in for extra flavour.

3 Add the garlic, anchovies, and half the capers, and beat again. The mixture will become a very thick green paste.

4 Gradually beat in the rest of the olive oil a little at a time and then season to taste with salt and pepper. Shortly before serving, stir in the lemon juice and zest, and add the reserved herbs and capers. Use soon or cover, chill, and use within 24 hours.

Capers
Preserved capers are a versatile kitchen essential, great with oily fish and boiled meats.

AÏOLI

Serve this garlic mayonnaise in the traditional Provençal way – with steamed vegetables, hard-boiled eggs, and poached fish.

MAKES 300ML (10FL OZ) **PREP** 20 MINS **REST** 10 MINS

2 large fresh garlic cloves, smashed and peeled
sea salt and freshly ground black pepper

1 very fresh large egg yolk
200ml (7fl oz) mild olive oil

1 Using a pestle and mortar, pound the garlic with a small pinch of salt. Add the egg yolk and season with pepper. Beat for 1 minute and then leave to rest for 5 minutes. Beat in the oil, a few drops at a time, as for a mayonnaise.

2 Once the sauce has emulsified, pour in the olive oil in a thin trickle, beating always with the pestle in the same direction. The sauce is ready once it has a very thick texture and the pestle almost stands up by itself in the bowl.

3 Cover and refrigerate for up to 24 hours until ready to use.

HERB MAYONNAISE

This green aromatic mayonnaise is great with asparagus, tender-stem broccoli, calabrese, or cauliflower.

SERVES 4–6 **MAKES** 300ML (10FL OZ) **PREP** 20 MINS **REST** 10 MINS

1 very fresh egg yolk
1 tsp Dijon mustard
sea salt and freshly ground black pepper
1 garlic clove, crushed
150ml (5fl oz) vegetable oil, such as groundnut, rapeseed, or sunflower
1 tbsp chopped basil

1 tbsp finely chopped flatleaf parsley
1 tbsp chopped tarragon or dill fronds
½ tbsp chopped coriander
1 sprig marjoram or oregano, leaves only
1 tbsp capers, drained
100ml (3½fl oz) fruity olive oil
1 tbsp red wine vinegar

1 Put the egg yolk, mustard, and a little salt in the bowl of a blender or food processor. Beat with a fork. Leave to rest for 5 minutes.

2 Add the garlic and pulse a few times. With the motor running, trickle in the vegetable oil. As the mixture thickens, add the vegetable oil a little faster.

3 Once you have added all the vegetable oil, slowly feed in half the herbs and the capers. Add the olive oil, then the red wine vinegar. Stop the motor.

4 Spoon the sauce into a bowl. Taste and adjust the seasoning. Leave to rest for 5 minutes. Stir in the remaining herbs. Gradually stir in about 2 tbsp of cold water to loosen the sauce slightly. This will keep for 24 hours covered and chilled, but stir in the remaining herbs and chilled water just before serving.

CHIMICHURRI

A favourite in Argentina, this sauce is served with dishes as diverse as barbecued beef and empanadas.

MAKES 200–250ML (7–8FL OZ) **PREP** 15 MINS **COOK** 15 MINS **INFUSE** 30 MINS

100ml (3½oz) fruity olive oil
2 garlic cloves, smashed, peeled, and crushed
2 tbsp sherry vinegar or red wine vinegar
1 shallot, finely chopped

4 tbsp chopped flatleaf parsley
½ tsp dried marjoram or oregano
½ tsp smoked paprika
sea salt and freshly ground black pepper

1 Whisk or beat all the ingredients except the salt and pepper together in a small bowl and then season with salt and pepper.
2 Transfer to a clean serving bowl, cover and keep in a cool place for 2 hours before serving. Adjust the seasoning at the last minute. Chimichurri can be refrigerated for up to 48 hours.

YOGHURT SAUCE WITH PARSLEY AND MINT

Keep this soothing sauce to hand as a cooling side dish for hot spicy foods.

MAKES 175ML (6FL OZ) **PREP** 20 MINS **STAND** 2 HOURS

150ml (5fl oz) natural yoghurt (not fat-free)
garlic clove, smashed, peeled, and crushed
1 tsp lemon juice
1 heaped tbsp chopped flatleaf parsley, plus 2 tsp to finish
10g (¼oz) feta cheese, mashed

1 tsp chopped summer savory or marjoram
1 tsp dried mint, plus 1 tsp to finish
sea salt and freshly ground black pepper
1½ tbsp fruity olive oil, to finish

1 Put the yoghurt, garlic, lemon juice, parsley, feta cheese, savory or marjoram, and dried mint in the small bowl of a food processor. Whiz until smooth. Season with salt and pepper to taste.
2 Transfer to a bowl, cover, and keep in a cool place for 2 hours before serving. At the last minute, adjust the seasoning, and scatter over the extra parsley and mint. Drizzle over the olive oil and stir it in gently.

Cook's note Yoghurt sauces can be refrigerated for up to 48 hours. If the sauce then looks too thick, stir in a little cold water to thin it down.

Variations You can vary the mixture of fresh and dried herbs, always scattering over a few extra fresh leaves just before serving. If you like, you can also replace the feta cheese with the same amount of tahini paste.

HOT SAUCES

If you want to make the most of herbs in a hot sauce, keep the sauce simple to let the herbal flavours really come through. Melted butter, a little stock, cream, or white wine are good partners for herbs.

FRESH SAGE SAUCE

This sauce is ideal with pork chops or escalopes, chicken, or turkey.

MAKES 250ML (8FL OZ) **PREP** 10 MINS **COOK** 10 MINS

2 bay leaves
125ml (4fl oz) chicken or vegetable stock
125ml (4fl oz) dry white wine
1 small sprig thyme
1 tbsp plain flour

20g (¾oz) slightly softened butter, plus
 15g (½oz) chilled butter, diced, to finish
1 tbsp chopped sage leaves, plus
 3–5 small leaves to finish
sea salt and freshly ground black pepper

1 Bruise the bay leaves with the back of a large knife or a kitchen mallet. Place in a pan over medium heat with the stock, wine, and thyme, and bring to a simmer.
2 Mash together the flour and softened butter in a cup or on a saucer using a fork until well mixed.
3 Whisk the butter and flour into the simmering liquid. Continue whisking for 3 minutes over a fast simmer, until the liquid has slightly thickened.
4 Reduce the heat. Remove the bay leaves and thyme. Add the sage and stir for 2 minutes. Remove from the heat, cool for 2 minutes, and then season with salt and pepper.
5 Whisk in the diced chilled butter, stir in the whole sage leaves, and serve.

Sage
Fresh sage is unbeatable with buttery risotto, while dried sage is delicious in stuffings.

PLAIN AND SIMPLE GARLIC SAUCE

Roasted garlic makes a fragrant sauce that works wonders with roasted meats.

MAKES 200–250ML (7–8FL OZ) **PREP** 15 MINS **COOK** 15 MINS **INFUSE** 30 MINS

2 heads fresh garlic, broken into unpeeled cloves
2 tbsp olive oil

150ml (5fl oz) single cream
sea salt and freshly ground black pepper

1 Preheat the oven to 130°C (250°F/Gas ½). Put the garlic cloves on a plate, drizzle with the olive oil, and rub it all over the cloves. Line a roasting pan with foil, add the cloves, and cover loosely with foil. Place in the oven and roast for about 1 hour, until the garlic becomes very soft.
2 Take out of the oven and tip the cloves onto a plate. Once cool, squeeze each clove to push out the pulp into a bowl. Mash it briefly with a fork.
3 Warm the cream in a small pan placed over a low heat. Take off the heat and thoroughly whisk in the mashed garlic pulp. Season with salt and pepper to taste and reheat gently until very hot but not quite simmering. Leftover sauce can be covered and refrigerated for up to a day.

Variations Stir in 1 tsp ground cumin or coriander and/or 2 tsp grated root ginger. Replace the cream with the same quantity of strained full-fat yoghurt, or also with stock, whisking in 20g (¾oz) diced chilled butter to finish off the sauce.

MELTED BUTTER AND CHERVIL SAUCE

Make this delicate sauce at the last minute and serve with salmon, sole, asparagus, or broccoli.

MAKES 120ML (4FL OZ) **PREP** 10 MINS **COOK** 15–20 MINS

1 scant tbsp cornflour
65g (2oz) chilled butter, diced
2 tsp lemon juice

1 heaped tbsp finely chopped chervil
sea salt and freshly ground white pepper

1 In a pan, whisk the cornflour with 120ml (4fl oz) water, and season with salt. Stir over a moderate heat until very hot but not boiling.
2 Whisk in the butter one piece at a time, without allowing the sauce to boil. Take off the heat and stir in the lemon juice and chervil. Season to taste with salt and white pepper and serve immediately.

Variations Whisk in 1 tbsp double cream at the last minute to make the sauce extra rich. You can also replace the chervil with the same quantity of finely chopped tarragon, dill fronds, or sorrel.

SOUPS

Fresh and dried herbs can be used to great effect in soups, whether in a modest supporting role or as the star of the show. Use dried herbs early in the cooking and snip in plenty of fresh herbs to finish off.

SORREL AND PEA SOUP

This smooth pea soup is given a distinctive edge with the sharp taste of sorrel.

SERVES 4–6 **PREP** 15 MINS **COOK** 30 MINS

1 tbsp sunflower, groundnut, or rapeseed oil
20g (¾oz) soft butter, plus 20g (¾oz) chilled diced butter
500g (1lb 2oz) shelled peas, fresh or frozen
1 floury potato, peeled and cut into small dice
2 flatleaf parsley sprigs, chopped
4 tbsp loosely packed small sorrel leaves, plus extra sorrel chopped, to garnish
sea salt and freshly ground black pepper
750ml (1¼ pints) vegetable or chicken stock
3 tbsp single cream, plus extra to garnish

1 Put the oil and the soft butter in a large pan placed over a medium heat. Add the peas, potato, parsley, and half of the sorrel leaves. Stir well for 2 minutes, then reduce the heat a little. Add 100ml (3½fl oz) water, and season lightly with salt and pepper. Partly cover and cook over a very low heat, stirring occasionally, for 15 minutes until the potato is tender. Remove from the heat and let cool a little.
2 Transfer to a food processor (or use a stick blender placed directly in the pan) and whiz until puréed. Return to the pan and stir in the stock. Bring to a simmer over a medium heat, stirring frequently. Reduce the heat a little and leave to simmer gently for 5 minutes. Taste, adjust the seasoning, and stir in the remaining sorrel leaves and the single cream.
3 Return to a low simmer, and whisk in the chilled diced butter. Adjust the seasoning and spoon into bowls. Decorate with a swirl of cream and a little chopped sorrel. Serve immediately.

Sorrel
With its somewhat bitter, sour flavour, sorrel is particularly good with fish, cream, and eggs.

CREAM OF HERB SOUP

You can use any combination of herbs you like for this verdant soup.

SERVES 4 **PREP** 15 MINS **COOK** 1 HOUR

2 tbsp butter
30g (1oz) each chopped onion and carrots
50g (1¾oz) each diced celery and spring onion
20g (¾oz) diced parsley root
20g (¾oz) plain flour
sea salt and freshly ground black pepper
1 litre (1¾ pints) chicken stock

2 garlic cloves, finely chopped
1 bay leaf
5 black peppercorns
120ml (4fl oz) single cream
6 tbsp chopped herbs, such as sage, basil, parsley, chervil, sorrel, lovage, oregano, thyme, or chives, in any combination

1 Place a medium pan over a low heat and add 1 tbsp butter. Add the onion, cover, and leave to sweat for about 5–10 minutes. Add the vegetables and stir to coat in butter. Cover and sweat until softened, about 5–10 minutes.
2 Sprinkle the flour over the vegetables and give them a stir. Season lightly, then pour in the stock. Raise the heat to high and bring the soup to a boil.
3 When it is boiling, turn down the heat and add the garlic, bay leaf, and peppercorns. Simmer uncovered for about 30 minutes. Skim off any froth.
4 Stir in the cream. Turn up the heat but do not boil. After 5 minutes, remove from the heat and strain the soup into a large bowl. Discard the vegetables and spices. Pour the soup back into the pan. Whisk in the rest of the butter and add the herbs, keeping some back to finish. Simmer for 5 minutes, stirring occasionally. Season to taste, spoon into bowls, and serve.

GUACAMOLE SOUP

Creamy-textured avocados blend in well with strongly flavoured herbs.

SERVES 4 **PREP** 15 MINS **CHILL** 1 HOUR **FINISH** 5 MINS

3 ripe Hass avocados, halved, pitted, and peeled
juice of 1 lime, plus 4 lime wedges for serving
2 tsp finely chopped lovage, plus 1 tsp to finish
2 spring onions, chopped
2 tbsp flatleaf parsley, chopped
3 tbsp picked watercress leaves

sea salt and freshly ground black pepper
1 tsp ground cumin
1 tsp coriander seeds, crushed
1 tbsp finely chopped coriander
800ml (1¼ pints) light vegetable stock

1 Chop the avocados and place in the bowl of a blender or food processor. Add the lime juice, lovage, spring onion, parsley, and watercress. Season, add the cumin and coriander, and whiz briefly. Add the stock slowly with the motor running.
2 Transfer to a bowl, cover, and chill for at least 1 hour or for up to 24 hours until needed. Serve chilled, sprinkled with the reserved lovage and the lime wedges.

TARATOR SOUP

Serve this cool, refreshing herb, yoghurt, and walnut soup in chunky glasses to start a meal on a hot summer's day.

SERVES 4 **PREP** 20 MINS **CHILL** 2 HOURS

600ml (1 pint) whole or semi-skimmed
   goat's or ewe's milk
3 tbsp finely chopped flatleaf parsley
1½ tbsp finely chopped dill fronds
1½ tbsp finely chopped coriander
2 tsp finely chopped mint
1 sprig thyme

4 tbsp fresh walnut kernels
250ml (8fl oz) natural yoghurt
small pinch of dried chilli or a few drops
   Tabasco sauce
sea salt and freshly ground black pepper
small bunch of dill fronds, chopped

1 Put the milk in a bowl, add 2 tbsp parsley, 1 tbsp each dill and coriander, 1 tsp mint, and the thyme sprig. Stir and refrigerate for 1 hour.

2 Put the walnuts in a pan of lightly salted boiling water, blanch for a minute, drain, crush lightly, and reserve.

3 Remove the thyme from the milk and discard. Pour the milk and herbs into the bowl of a blender or food processor. With the motor running, add the walnuts a few at a time so they are thoroughly chopped. Then pour in the yoghurt, and add the dried chilli or Tabasco sauce, and blend well. Season with salt and pepper to taste. Return to the fridge for 1 hour, or even overnight, until ready to serve.

4 To finish, stir in the reserved herbs, and the small bunch of dill fronds, and adjust the seasoning. Float in a few ice cubes and serve immediately.

Thyme
*One of the most useful of all
herbs, aromatic thyme is
indispensable fresh or dried.*

TOPPINGS

Finely chopped herbs make lovely bread toppings and create wonderful fragrant crusts for baked dishes. They can also be lightly stirred into dishes cooked on the hob to top them off with a fresh zingy kick.

ROSEMARY, GARLIC, AND OLIVE TOPPING

For another scented bread, replace the rosemary with thyme, or 2 tbsp mixed aniseed or fennel seeds, and use sun-dried tomatoes instead of olives.

FOR 800G (1¾LB) DOUGH SERVES 8–10 PREP 20 MINS REST 30 MINS COOK 25–30 MINS

100ml (3½fl oz) fruity olive oil
6 garlic cloves, peeled and cut into slivers
500g (1lb 2oz) packet white bread mix
16 black olives, pitted and chopped

5 stalks rosemary, about 7.5cm (3in) long, leaves stripped, stalks discarded
coarse sea salt and freshly ground black pepper

1 Put some kitchen paper onto a plate. Pour the olive oil into a pan over a low heat. Add the garlic. Cook for 2 minutes until softened but not coloured. Lift out the garlic and spread it on the kitchen paper. Let the oil and garlic cool.

2 Make the bread according to the instructions. When it is ready, knock the air out of it. Spread the dough into an oiled 30 x 22cm (12 x 8in) baking tray and flatten gently.

3 Drizzle 1 tbsp of the cold garlicky oil over the dough, and spread it round. Scatter over the garlic, olives, and rosemary and pat in lightly. Drizzle over 1–2 tbsp of the oil. Cover loosely with cling film and let rest for 30 minutes.

4 Preheat the oven to 190°C (375°F/Gas 5). Remove the cling film and place the tray in the oven. Bake for 20–25 minutes. Let cool, season, and drizzle over the remaining oil.

MANAKEISH

This fragrant lemony topping for bread is popular in the Middle East.

FOR 800G (1¾LB) DOUGH SERVES 8–10 PREP 20 MINS REST 30 MINS COOK 25–30 MINS

3 tbsp lemon thyme
1 tsp ground sumac
1 tsp dried mint
2 garlic cloves, crushed

1 tbsp coarsely grated lemon zest
1 tbsp lemon juice
5 tbsp fruity olive oil
500g (1lb 2oz) packet white bread mix

1 Pound, mash, or whiz all the topping ingredients together.

2 Make the bread according to the instructions. When it is ready, knock the air out of it. Spread the dough into an oiled 30 x 22cm (12 x 8in) baking tray and flatten gently.

3 Spread the topping over the bread, leave to rest, and bake as above.

SWEET IDEAS

Many herbs, especially mint, basil, and coriander, add a lovely distinctive note to custards, syrups, and fruit desserts. Use in small amounts: too little is better than too much as the aromatic strength of herbs can easily overpower a delicate sweet concoction.

BASIL AND VANILLA CUSTARD

Drizzle this infused custard over strawberry tarts, crumbles, and fruit snacks.

SERVES 4–6 **PREP** 20 MINS **COOK** 30 MINS PLUS COOLING

500ml (16fl oz) whole milk
3 tbsp loosely packed basil leaves, plus a few small
    leaves to decorate
2 vanilla pods
3 large or 4 medium fresh egg yolks

6 tbsp caster sugar
1 tsp cornflour
3 tbsp crème fraîche
Szechuan pepper (optional), to garnish

1 Put the milk in a pan. Squash the basil leaves with your hands, and add them to the milk. Split the vanilla pods lengthways and scrape out the black pulpy seeds. Put the pods and seeds in the pan. Bring to a simmer over a low heat, stirring occasionally with a wooden spoon. As soon as the milk starts to bubble, reduce the heat as low as possible, and cook very gently, stirring frequently, for 10 minutes. Take off the heat and set aside.

2 In a large bowl, whisk together the egg yolks and the sugar until smooth and pale. Whisk in the cornflour.

3 Place a fine sieve over the bowl, and strain the hot milk a little at a time into the yolk and sugar mixture. Push down the basil and vanilla into the sieve to extract as much flavour as possible. Whisk the yolk mixture well between additions. Discard the vanilla pod and basil after sieving.

4 Return the mixture to the pan over a very low heat. Bring to a gentle simmer, stirring constantly for 10 minutes or until the custard has thickened enough to coat the back of the spoon. Do not allow it to boil. If necessary take it off the heat from time to time.

5 Leave to get cold, stirring occasionally. Stir in the crème fraîche and once the custard is completely cold, place it in the fridge to chill further.

6 Serve well chilled, decorated with small basil leaves. If you like, you can grind a little Szechuan pepper over the custard before serving to bring out the mild pepperiness of the basil.

MINT AND ORANGE SYRUP

This syrup is lovely for flavouring juleps, cocktails, Pimm's, and wine cups.

MAKES 250ML (8FL OZ)   **PREP** 15 MINS   **COOK** 20 MINS

5 tbsp chopped mint, preferably Moroccan mint
grated zest from 1–2 large unwaxed oranges
300g (10oz) caster sugar

100ml (3½fl oz) freshly squeezed orange juice
2 tbsp Cointreau or other orange liqueur

You will need: 2 pieces of clean **muslin**, dampened; **string**; fine **sieve**; **funnel**; sterilized 250ml (8fl oz) **bottle or jar** (see p176) with a stopper or lid

1 Put the mint and grated orange zest in a double layer of muslin, bring up the edges, and tie with string (see p129). Put the sugar, orange juice, orange liqueur, and 200ml (7fl oz) water in a pan, and add the muslin bag.
2 Bring to the boil over a moderate heat, stirring occasionally until the sugar has dissolved. Leave to simmer for 5–7 minutes, stirring from time to time until the syrup has thickened just a little.
3 Remove from the heat, cover, and leave to get cold. Lift out the muslin bag and squeeze it over the pan to extract as much flavour as possible, then discard it. Strain the syrup through a fine sieve lined with dampened muslin into a sterilized bottle and seal. Store in a cool place and use within 4–6 weeks.

LAVENDER SYRUP

Try with baked apples, roasted apricots, poached peaches, and creamy yoghurt.

MAKES 200–250ML (7–8FL OZ)   **PREP** 15 MINS   **COOK** 15 MINS   **INFUSE** 30 MINS

2 tsp dried lavender flowers
300g (10oz) caster sugar

pared zest of 1 small unwaxed lemon, cut into small strips

You will need: piece of clean **muslin**, dampened; fine **sieve; funnel**; sterilized 250ml (8fl oz) **bottle or jar** (see p178) with a stopper or lid

1 Put the dried lavender flowers, sugar, and lemon zest strips into a saucepan with 300ml (10fl oz) water. Place over a medium heat and stir.
2 Once the sugar has dissolved after 3–4 minutes, stop stirring and remove from the heat. Leave to infuse for at least 30 minutes, stirring occasionally.
3 Place the pan over a medium heat and bring to the boil without stirring. Turn the heat to high and let bubble for 5–7 minutes until thickened.
4 Remove from the heat. When the syrup is cool enough to handle, strain slowly and carefully into a sterilized bottle through a fine sieve lined with dampened muslin. Leave to get absolutely cold, seal, and store in a cool place. Use within 4–6 weeks.

CORDIALS

The delicate flavours of herbs make wonderful, refreshing cordials, which you can enjoy long after the growing season. Always use scrupulously clean utensils to minimize the risk of fermentation.

BLACKCURRANT CORDIAL

A couple of tablespoons of this cordial added to a glass of sparkling mineral water makes a perfect summer's day thirst quencher.

MAKES 950ML (1⅔ PINTS) **PREP** 20 MINS

450g (1lb) blackcurrants
225g (8oz) sugar

zest and juice of 1 well-washed
unwaxed lemon

You will need: piece of clean **muslin**, dampened; **funnel**; sterilized 1 litre (1¾ pint) **bottle or jar** (see p176) with a stopper or lid

1 Place the blackcurrants, sugar, and 250ml (8fl oz) water in a pan over a low heat. Bring to a simmer, stirring occasionally. Gently mash the blackcurrants to make sure that all of the berries have broken open. Cook for 5–8 minutes, until the sugar has dissolved and the blackcurrants have yielded their juice.
2 Stir in the lemon juice and zest and remove the pan from the heat.
3 Slowly strain the contents of the pan through a funnel lined with dampened muslin into a sterilized bottle. Allow the liquid to cool, then seal and refrigerate. Use within 6–8 weeks.

Blackcurrants
*Packed with vitamin C,
blackcurrants are great
for cordials and juices.*

ELDERFLOWER CORDIAL

Either dilute this fragrant cordial in sparkling mineral water, or use as a flavouring in ice cream or other sweet dishes.

MAKES 950ML (1⅔ PINTS) **PREP** 20 MINS **INFUSE** 48 HOURS

450g (1lb) sugar
2 unwaxed lemons, well washed

15 large elderflower heads in full flower, shaken to dislodge any insects
15g (½oz) citric acid

You will need: piece of clean **muslin**, dampened; **sieve; funnel**; sterilized 1 litre (1¾ pint) **bottle or jar** (see below) with a stopper or lid

1 Place the sugar in a large bowl and pour 750ml (1¼ pints) boiling water over it. Stir until the sugar dissolves, then set aside.
2 Grate the zest from the lemons and add to the sugar water. Then slice the lemons thickly and add them to the sugar water as well.
3 Submerge the elderflower heads in the sugar water and lemon mixture. Add the citric acid and stir to dissolve. Cover and set aside for 48 hours to infuse.
4 Line a sieve with a piece of dampened muslin and set over a large bowl. Carefully filter the cordial through the sieve. Place a funnel into the neck of a sterilized bottle and slowly pour the cordial into it. Seal the lid and store in a cool, dark place. Once opened, store in the fridge for up to 3 weeks.

To sterilize bottles and jars, preheat the oven to 130°C/250°F/Gas Mark ½. Wash the bottles or jars in soapy water. Rinse well, and then drain. Place upright in the oven for 15 minutes before using. You can also sterilize glass containers by running them through a hot cycle of the dishwasher.

Elderflower
Floral-scented elderflowers make the most refreshing cordials when pure white.

ANGELICA LIQUEUR

Vodka absorbs the flavour of the herbs in this spicy liqueur that packs a punch.

MAKES 360ML (12FL OZ) **PREP** 30 MINS **INFUSE** 3–6 MONTHS

2 cardamom seeds, crushed
1 tsp dried marjoram, crumbled
pinch each of ground allspice, ground star anise,
  ground cinnamon, and ground coriander
360ml (12fl oz) vodka

120ml (4fl oz) sugar syrup using 160g
  (5½oz) sugar to 80ml (2¾fl oz) water
2 tbsp finely chopped angelica root,
  washed and thoroughly dried

You will need: piece of clean **muslin**, dampened; **sieve**; sterilized 750ml (1¼ pint)
jar with a lid, 1 small sterilized **jar** with a lid, plus 1 sterilized decorative 750ml
(1¼ pint) **bottle** (see opposite) with stopper

1 Crush the cardamom in a mortar and pestle and place in the larger sterilized jar.
Add the marjoram, allspice, star anise, cinnamon, and coriander. Pour in 4 tbsp of
the vodka. Seal and store in a cool dark place for 7 days.
2 After 7 days, filter the mixture through a sieve lined with dampened muslin into
a bowl. Add the sugar syrup and 250ml (8fl oz) of the vodka. Re-sterilize the jar, add
the liqueur mixture, and close the lid. Set aside in a cool, dark place for 2 weeks.
3 In a separate small sterilized jar with a lid, place the chopped angelica root and
add the remaining 4 tbsp of vodka. Close the lid tightly and store in a cool, dark
place. After 2 weeks, strain the liquid as before, pressing down gently on the
angelica root. Add the angelica extract to the herb-spice liqueur
by ½ teaspoons until you achieve the flavour you like.
4 Store the remaining angelica extract, if any, and the liqueur
in their closed jars in a cool, dark place for 2 months, then taste
the liqueur. Add more angelica extract if you like. Pour into a
sterilized decorative bottle, close tightly, and store for 3 more
months for the best developed flavour.

Angelica
To dry angelica root, cut it into
long strips and dry overnight in
the oven on a very low heat.

HERBAL TEAS

There's something immensely satisfying about making herbal teas using herbs or seeds you have grown and harvested yourself. Herbal teas are regarded by some as nature's medicine and there is no denying the power of a cup of herbal tea to relax or uplift you, depending on the herb you choose.

MAKING TEA

After harvesting your herbs give them a rinse, blot them on kitchen paper, then chop them finely (see p123). To use your own dried herbs, see p114. Here is a general guide for making herbal tea.

1 You will need either 2 tbsp of finely chopped fresh herbs or 1 tbsp of finely crumbled dried herbs for every cup of tea you wish to make. Place in a teapot.

2 Bring to the boil enough water to fill your cups. The instant the water reaches the boil, pour it on the herbs. Water boiled for too long makes flat-tasting tea.

3 Steep the herbs in the teapot for 5 minutes. If you want your tea to be stronger, use more herbs rather than a longer steeping time.

4 Warm the tea cups by running them under hot water for a few moments, and empty them. Then pour the tea through a strainer into the cups.

5 You can add 1 tsp of honey or sugar, or a squeeze of lemon to flavour the tea to taste, or serve it without any additional ingredients. Ideally, the tea cups and teapot should be non-metallic. Enamelled metal will do, but glass is better. Very best of all are ceramic or porcelain tea cups and teapots.

ICED TEA

Coldness dulls the palate, so make your iced tea about one-third stronger than your ordinary cup of hot herbal tea, and allow the tea to cool before adding it to the ice cubes. Use herbs with mint and lemon flavours, such as spearmint and lemongrass, to create extra refreshing cold drinks.

1 Make enough herbal tea to freeze some in ice cube trays while the rest chills in the fridge. Using herbal tea ice cubes in your iced tea avoids diluting the tea.

3 Garnish your iced tea with a fresh sprig of the same herb you used to make the tea. You can also add slices of lemon, lime, or orange.

2 Once they have frozen solid (after about 2 hours) pop the herbal tea ice cubes out of the tray and place them in a tall glass. Pour over the cooled herbal tea.

MAKING A DECOCTION

A decoction is used for tougher herbs, such as juniper berries and angelica root. Pour 500ml (16fl oz) of water into a pan and add 2–4 heaped tsp of chopped, crushed, or grated herbs. Bring to a boil, cover, and reduce the heat. Simmer for 20 minutes, turn off the heat, and steep for 10 minutes. Strain and serve, or refrigerate in a sealed jar for 1 week.

HOW TO MAKE TEA BAGS

The great advantage of making tea bags using herbs you've grown and dried yourself (see p114) is that you can control the quality and the taste. Make the tea bags as you need them, or prepare them ahead of time. When used in tea, dried herbs are about twice as potent as fresh herbs.

1 Tip the dried herb of your choice out of its storage jar and gently crumble the leaves or flower heads. Use a single herb, or create your own blend of herbs.

2 Cut a 10 x 10cm (4 x 4in) muslin square. Place 1 tbsp of dried herbs in the middle of the muslin. This will be enough for a single cup of herbal tea.

3 Bring up the corners of the muslin to enclose the dried herbs. Hold the corners together and tie them securely with a piece of kitchen string.

4 Place the bag in the cup and pour on the boiling water. Allow the tea to steep for five minutes, or until it suits your taste, remove the tea bag, and serve.

MOROCCAN MINT TEA

This sweet mint tea accompanies most meals all across North Africa, not just in Morocco. Its ubiquity doesn't detract from its delicacy.

SERVES 8

3 tbsp loose green tea or 5 tea bags of green tea
1 bunch fresh Moroccan mint or spearmint

2 litres (3½ pints) water
200g (7oz) caster sugar

1 Place the green tea and fresh mint into a large teapot.
2 Pour the water into a large pan over high heat. Bring to boiling, then pour it carefully into the teapot. Steep for 5 minutes, stirring gently once or twice. Add the sugar and stir until it dissolves.
3 Pour the hot tea through a strainer into serving cups, or cool and pour over ice cubes in glasses for iced mint tea.

ROSEHIP TEA

During World War II, when oranges from the continent were scarce, British schoolchildren were given rosehip syrup for their daily dose of vitamin C. The tea is light and tangy.

SERVES 2

7 large hips of *Rosa rugosa*, stems removed
480ml (16fl oz) water

1 Coarsely chop the rosehips, including the seeds, and place in a teapot.
2 Pour the water into a pan over high heat or into a kettle and bring to boiling. Pour over the rosehips.
3 Steep for 10 minutes, strain, and serve in warmed cups.

SWEET VIOLET TEA

This was a great favourite in Britain during the reign of Queen Victoria. Float a fresh sweet violet in each cup for extra flavour and a charming garnish.

SERVES 3

18 sweet violets, picked over and gently rinsed
750ml (1¼ pints) water

1 Place the sweet violets in a teapot.
2 Pour the water into a pan over high heat or into a kettle and bring to boiling. Immediately pour it into the teapot and stir gently.
3 Steep for 10 minutes and then pour through a strainer into warmed cups.

CHAMOMILE TEA

One of the most popular herbal teas in the world today, chamomile was enjoyed by the ancient Egyptians and early Romans. It is both relaxing and reviving.

SERVES 3

3 heaped tbsp fresh chamomile flowers
750ml (1¼ pints) water
honey to taste (optional)

1 Place the chamomile flowers in a teapot.
2 Pour the water into a pan over high heat or into a kettle and bring to boiling. Immediately pour into the teapot. Steep for 5–10 minutes.
3 Pour the tea through a strainer into warmed cups. Add honey to taste and stir, or drink it unsweetened.

TILLEUL TEA

Europe's famous linden tree (*Tilia europaea*) is also known as the lime tree. Its flowers make a delightful, relaxing tea with a light, floral scent.

SERVES 3

9 linden flowers
750ml (1¼ pints) water
1½ tsp honey

1 Place the linden flowers in a teapot.
2 Pour the water into a pan over high heat or into a kettle and bring to boiling. Immediately pour it into the teapot and add the honey.
3 Steep for 5 minutes, then strain into warmed cups

FOUR-HERB DIGESTIF TEA

A digestif is, as you can tell by its name, an aid to digestion. Here's one to make straight from your own herb garden. This keeps in the fridge for up to 6 days.

SERVES 4

2 tbsp each peppermint, fennel fronds, lemon balm, and chamomile flowers, roughly chopped
1 litre (1¾ pints) water
honey to taste (optional)

1 Place the chopped herbs in a teapot.
2 Pour the water into a pan over high heat or into a kettle and bring to boiling. Immediately pour it into the teapot.
3 Steep for 10 minutes, then strain into warmed cups.

LAVENDER AND LEMON VERBENA TEA

Lemon verbena on its own makes a lovely, lemony tea, but when it is paired with the floral scent of lavender, something special happens.

SERVES 6

140g (5oz) lemon verbena leaves, loosely torn
3 tbsp lavender flower heads
1.5 litres (2¾ pints) water

1 Tear up the lemon verbena leaves and place in a bowl. Add the lavender flower heads and stir to mix. Place in a large teapot. (For a single serving of tea, use 1 tsp of each herb in a cup.)
2 Pour the water into a pan over a high heat and bring to boiling, then pour it into the teapot (or cup). Steep for 5 minutes.
3 Pour through a strainer into warmed cups (for a single cup, strain into another cup).

SAGE AND LEMON BALM TEA

By itself, sage has a rather strong, herbaceous flavour, which is much more palatable when combined with lemon balm.

SERVES 2

2 tbsp sage, finely chopped
3 tbsp lemon balm, finely chopped

480ml (16fl oz) water
1 tsp honey

1 Place the sage and lemon balm in a teapot.
2 Pour the water into a pan over high heat or into a kettle and bring to boiling. Immediately pour it into the teapot. Add the honey and stir. Steep for 10–15 minutes.
3 Pour the tea through a strainer into warmed cups.

FRESH GINGER TEA

This is a favourite tea during the cold and flu season but it's reviving any time.

SERVES 4

5cm (2in) fresh root ginger, peeled and
thinly sliced
1 litre (1¾ pints) water

1 tsp honey
4 lemon slices

1 Bring the water just to a boil in a pan over high heat. Add the ginger slices, cover, and reduce the heat. Simmer for 15 minutes.
2 Add the honey and stir to dissolve.
3 Strain into warmed cups, add a slice of lemon to each, and serve.

BERGAMOT TEA

The leaves and flowers of bergamot have a citrus fragrance and flavour
Bergamot tea with a squeeze of lemon makes refreshing iced tea.

SERVES 3

2 tbsp bergamot leaves and flowers,
 finely chopped
750ml (1¼ pints) water

honey to taste
3 lemon slices

1 Place the bergamot leaves and flowers in a teapot.
2 Pour the water into a pan over high heat or into a kettle and bring to boiling.
Immediately pour it into the teapot. Stir in a little honey to taste.
3 Steep for 5–10 minutes, depending on the strength you desire. Pour through
a strainer into warmed cups. Garnish each cup with a slice of lemon.

ANISE HYSSOP AND CALAMINT TEA

Anise hyssop and calamint each make delightful teas on their own, but together
play strongly on a mint theme with a light note of liquorice in the background.

SERVES 3

1 tbsp anise hyssop, finely chopped
1 tbsp calamint leaves and stem, finely chopped

750ml (1¼ pints) water
honey to taste

1 Place the herbs in a teapot.
2 Pour the water into a pan over high heat or into a kettle and bring to boiling.
Immediately pour it into the teapot. Add a little honey to taste. Steep for 5 minutes
or longer if you like it stronger.
3 Pour through a strainer into warmed cups.

ROSE-SCENTED GERANIUM TEA

This tea has long been used as a calming and stress-relieving drink. Other
scented geranium leaves can also be used to make different teas.

SERVES 4

185g (6½oz) rose-scented geranium leaves
1 litre (1¾ pints) water
honey to taste

1 Place the leaves in a teapot.
2 Pour the water into a pan over high heat or into a kettle and bring to boiling.
Immediately pour it into the teapot. Add honey to taste and stir.
3 Steep for 5 minutes, strain into warmed cups, and serve.

PARTNER CHARTS

Some herb and ingredient marriages – fennel and sea bass, basil and tomato, and egg and tarragon – are made in heaven. Others are less obvious but also exciting. These charts guide you to some different combinations worth trying.

MEAT

INGREDIENT	HERB PARTNERS	COOK'S NOTES
Beef	*Bouquet garni, Parsley, Bay leaf, Thyme, Lovage, Juniper berries, Horseradish, Orange, Chilli, Garlic, Welsh onion, Capers, Holy basil, Caraway seeds*	*A generous bouquet garni tied together with dried orange peel works wonders in slow-cooked beef dishes*
Lamb, mutton	*Rosemary, Lemon, Lime, Garlic, Basil, Lavender, Capers, Coriander, Mint, Fennel*	*Go easy on the rosemary with spring lamb; chop fresh mint and coriander and add to pan juices after roasting lamb*
Pork	*Garlic, Fennel seeds, Thyme, Sage, Parsley, Hyssop, Bay leaf, Curry leaf, Coriander, Marjoram, Bergamot, Holy basil, Caraway seeds*	*Use crushed fennel seeds with pork belly; before roasting, insert sage leaves and garlic slivers into cuts made in meat*
Veal	*Sage, Bay leaf, Parsley, Thyme, Savory, Capers, Lemon, Orange, Garlic, Lemon balm, Caraway seeds*	*Top osso bucco (veal casserole) with gremolata; use fresh thyme or savory for delicately poached veal blanquette*
Venison, furred game	*Bay leaf, Juniper berries, Fennel, Rosemary, Sage, Thyme, Parsley, Hyssop*	*Add plenty of mixed herbs to marinades for venison*

POULTRY

INGREDIENT	HERB PARTNERS	COOK'S NOTES
Chicken, poussin, turkey	*Parsley, Garlic, Chives, Bouquet garni, Tarragon, Dill, Smallage, Thyme, Lemon, Lime, Fennel, Sage, Chervil, Bergamot, Holy Basil, Pot marigold*	*Be generous – poultry can be on the bland side and responds well to aromatic assistance*
Duck	*Parsley, Garlic, Chives, Bouquet garni, Tarragon, Dill, Smallage, Thyme, Lemon, Orange*	
Goose	*Parsley, Garlic, Bouquet garni, Tarragon, Dill, Smallage, Thyme, Lemon, Bay leaf*	*Dried thyme is particularly good with goose fat*
Guinea fowl, pheasant, wild birds	*Parsley, Garlic, Bouquet garni, Chives, Tarragon, Dill, Smallage, Thyme, Lemon, Hyssop*	

FISH AND SHELLFISH

INGREDIENT	HERB PARTNERS	COOK'S NOTES
Haddock, cod, hake, pollock, hoki, monkfish	*Dill, Parsley, Thyme, Bay leaf, Sorrel, Lemon, Horseradish, Lemon basil, Pot marigold, Perilla, Sage, Rosemary*	*Be generous with thyme and parsley when flavouring smoked fish and serve with horseradish sauce*
Salmon, trout, skate, eel	*Dill, Parsley, Bay leaf, Capers, Orange, Lemon, Fennel, Horseradish, Lemon balm, Rosemary*	*Capers, butter, and a splash of wine vinegar are a classic accompaniment for skate*
Sardines, mackerel, tuna, herring	*Dill, Parsley, Sorrel, Rocket, Fennel, Lemon*	*Scatter plenty of herbs over fish before grilling, roasting, or pan-frying*
Sea bass, John Dory	*Fennel, Coriander, Lemongrass, Lemon, Lemon basil*	*Stuff plenty of herbs inside the cavity before roasting*
Sole, brill, plaice, halibut	*Parsley, Lemon, Lemon basil*	*The delicate flavour of these fish only requires a little parsley, lemon, and butter*
Red mullet, bream, Mediterranean fish	*Fennel, Parsley, Lemon, Orange, Lemon basil, Pot marigold*	
Mussels, clams, oysters	*Parsley, Garlic, Chives, Thyme, Fennel, Dill*	*Steam mussels in white wine flavoured with finely chopped mixed herbs*
Prawns, crab, lobster, squid	*Garlic, Ginger, Chives, Lemongrass, Lime, Coriander, Chilli, Parsley, Oregano*	

DAIRY

INGREDIENT	HERB PARTNERS	COOK'S NOTES
Eggs	*Parsley, Tarragon, Chervil, Dill, Chives, Welsh onion, Wild garlic, Thyme, Savory, Sweet cicely, Marjoram, Sorrel*	*Use finely chopped fresh fines herbes to flavour eggs; a little thyme or savory is good with a robust tortilla*
Cheese:		*Fresh, creamy cheeses respond well to finely chopped fines herbes; mature cheeses to a sprinkling of dried seeds; and cooked cheeses to mustard seeds*
Fresh, creamy	*Basil, Sage, Chives, Lemon balm, Marjoram*	
Semi-hard, hard	*Cumin seeds, Fennel seeds, Caraway seeds, Coriander seeds, Mustard seeds*	
Yoghurt, cream	*Parsley, Tarragon, Chervil, Dill, Chives, Mint, Coriander, Borage, Sorrel*	*Mix equal parts water and yoghurt with ice cubes and finely chopped coriander, chives, or parsley for a refreshing drink*

VEGETABLES, LEGUMES, AND WHEAT

INGREDIENT	HERB PARTNERS	COOK'S NOTES
Sweet peppers, aubergines, courgettes	Garlic, Chilli, Parsley, Coriander, Tarragon, Dill, Oregano, Marjoram	Raw or grilled courgettes are good with fresh tarragon and dill
Spinach	Garlic, Chilli, Lemon	Stir-fry and squeeze lemon over
Cabbage, cauliflower, broccoli, calabrese, Brussels sprouts	Parsley, Thyme, Savory, Garlic, Juniper berries, Capers, Fennel seeds, Coriander seeds, Caraway seeds, Bay leaf	Slow-cooked red cabbage and cured sauerkraut are particularly good with fennel seeds, coriander seeds, capers, and juniper berries
Green beans	Garlic, Parsley, Chervil, Coriander	
Oriental green vegetables	Garlic, Chives, Ginger, Ground coriander, Chilli, Cumin, Lemongrass	
Celery	Coriander seeds, Chives, Parsley	
Salad leaves	Fines herbes	Do not use with dried herbs
Mushrooms	Garlic, Chives, Parsley, Dill, Coriander	
Beetroot	Parsley, Chives, Coriander, Thyme	Use fresh herbs for boiled beetroot; dried thyme for roasted beetroot
Carrots	Garlic, Sage, Cumin, Bay leaf, Thyme, Dill, Fennel	
Potatoes	Garlic, Garlic chives, Wild garlic, Chives, Parsley, Thyme, Bay leaf, Rosemary, Sage, Dill, Mint, Chervil, Fines herbes	Use chopped fines herbes, dill, or mint on new potatoes; garlic, thyme, and Mediterranean herbs on roasted potatoes
Sweet potatoes	Garlic, Rosemary, Thyme, Bay leaf, Fennel seeds	
Swedes, parsnips, turnips, squashes	Parsley, Thyme, Rosemary, Garlic	Roasted vegetables thrive on garlic and strongly flavoured Mediterranean herbs
Globe artichokes	Chervil, Parsley, Garlic, Chives, Mint, Lovage, Smallage, Dill, Sorrel	Serve with a garlicky vinaigrette
Peas	Chervil, Parsley, Chives, Mint, Lovage, Smallage, Dill, Sorrel, Savory	
Beans (broad, dried, haricot), chickpeas	Bouquet garni, Savory, Garlic, Parsley, Lovage, Mint, Coriander, Bay leaf, Thyme, Marjoram, Oregano, Good King Henry, Cumin, Wild rocket	Drain beans after cooking with bouquet garni, then scatter with fresh herbs
Lentils	Garlic, Welsh onion, Parsley, Thyme, Bay leaf, Coriander, Savory	Finely chopped parsley is good with green lentils
Bulghur wheat	Coriander, Garlic, Parsley, Thyme, Mint	Add chopped herbs generously

FRUIT

Use herbs in moderation, as they can easily overpower the fragile flavour of fruit

INGREDIENT	HERB PARTNERS	COOK'S NOTES
Tomatoes	Basil, Marjoram, Oregano, Lovage, Tarragon, Coriander, Garlic, Chives	Tomato and tarragon is as good as tomato and basil
Avocados	Chives, Rocket, Lovage, Smallage, Sorrel, Coriander	
Apples	Lavender, Coriander, Fennel	
Pears	Rosemary , Lavender, Coriander	Use dried herbs very sparingly
Bananas	Lemon, Orange, Mint, Coriander, Lemongrass	
Peaches, nectarines, apricots, plums	Basil, Sweet cicely, Coriander, Lavender	Fresh herbs work better with poached fruit; use dried coriander and lavender in dried fruit compotes
Grapes	Coriander, Lemon	
Berries, cherries	Chocolate mint, Basil	Chocolate mint is lovely with raspberries; try chopped basil and a sprinkling of balsamic vinegar with strawberries
Melon	Mint, Basil, Coriander	
Rhubarb	Orange, Sweet cicely, Ginger	Cook in orange-scented sugar
Mangoes, pineapples, papayas, kiwi	Lemon, Mint, Basil, Coriander	Sprinkle grated citrus zest and finely chopped basil over sliced fruit
Citrus fruits	Lemongrass, Coriander	
Coconut	Chilli, Ginger, Garlic, Chives, Coriander, Thai basil	Herbs counteract the fattiness of coconut in cooked dishes
Figs	Coriander, Lavender	

DESSERTS AND SWEET THINGS

INGREDIENT	HERB PARTNERS	COOK'S NOTES
Pastries, biscuits, cakes	Dill seeds, Fennel seeds, Caraway seeds, Coriander seeds, Ginger, Lavender	
Custards, cream, ice cream	Bay leaf, Lavender, Coriander, Sweet cicely, Elder, Angelica, Chocolate mint, Cinnamon basil	Put the herbs in a muslin bag and infuse the custard milk
Chocolate	Ginger, Mint, Orange, Coriander, Lemongrass, Lemon, Fennel seeds, Rose petals	Use aromatic flavours sparingly with good quality chocolate

INDEX

A

aïoli 162
alecost 69
amaranth 23
angelica 24
  angelica liqueur 177
anise 58
anise hyssop 15, 22
  anise hyssop and calamint tea 185
aphids 99
avocados
  avocado, paprika, and lime salsa 148
  guacamole soup 168

B

bacterial diseases 100
balm of Gilead 34
basil 9, 12, 13, 52–3
  basil and vanilla custard 172
  citrus and basil marinade 143
  herb mayonnaise 162
  sauce verte 161
bay leaf 43, 77
  bay leaf, lovage, and juniper
    marinade 142
  horseradish and bay leaf coating 140
  sage, juniper, and bay leaf rub 137
bay sucker nymphs 99
beds, growing herbs in 83
bergamot 18, 46, 79, 80
  bergamot tea 185
blackcurrants 60, 106
  blackcurrant cordial 175
borage 26
bouquets garni 128
bread, toppings 171
bruising herbs 125
bulbs, dividing 91
bulghur wheat
  herb tabbouleh 152
butters 130–3

C

calamint 28
  anise hyssop and calamint tea 185
capers 30
  dill, watercress, caper, and
    tomato salsa 149
  parsley, caper,
    and olive vinaigrette 157

caraway 30
caterpillars 98
chamomile 17, 19, 31, 76
  chamomile tea 183
cheese
  rocket and mascarpone salsa 148
  spring herb salad with
    goat's cheese 153
chervil 11, 24
  melted butter and chervil sauce 165
  mushrooms à la Grecque 145
  salad with chervil and green beans 155
chicory 33
chilli peppers 29, 117, 126
  chilli, chive, and garlic dressing 156
  lemongrass and chilli salsa 147
chimichurri 163
chives 11, 20, 76
  chilli, chive, and garlic dressing 156
  courgette with chive marinade 145
chrysanthemum, edible 34
cicely, sweet 47
citrus fruit 36–7
  citrus and basil marinade 143
climate 76–9
coatings 139–41
compost 85
containers 80, 89, 92–3, 97
cordials 175–6
coriander 8, 14, 35
  coriander and mint coating 139
  dill and coriander coating 141
  mushrooms à la Grecque 145
courgette with chive marinade 145
cream of herb soup 168
cress, garden 50
cucumber with tarragon and cream 144
cumin 35
curry leaf 46, 78
custard, basil, and vanilla 172
cuttings 90

D

dandelion 69
  dandelion, rocket, and flower salad 151
decoctions 180
digestif tea 183
dill 10, 23
  dill and coriander coating 141

dill, watercress, caper, and
    tomato salsa 149
  dilled smoked haddock 144
diseases 100–1
dittany of Crete, oregano 55, 77
division 91
dressings 156
drinks 175–85
drying herbs 114–19

E

elder 66
elderflower cordial 176
endive, Belgian 33

F

fat hen 32
fennel 19, 40
  fennel and thyme rub 136
fenugreek 72
fertilizers 92–3
flavourings 128–9
flowers
  dandelion, rocket, and flower salad 151
  drying 117
  freezing 110
  harvesting 96, 106
four-herb digestif tea 183
freezing herbs 110–13
fridge, storing herbs in 108–9
fungal diseases 101

G

garlic 20, 21, 125
  aïoli 162
  chilli, chive, and garlic dressing 156
  frozen garlic roll 112–13
  plain and simple garlic sauce 165
  plaiting 118–19
  rosemary, garlic, and olive topping 171
  snail butter 133
  warm tomato and garlic vinaigrette 157
garlic chives 21
geranium 56, 78
  rose-scented geranium tea 185
ginger 73
  fresh ginger tea 184
good King Henry 32
grating roots 127
green beans, salad with chervil and 155

gremolata 137
growing herbs 75–99
guacamole soup 168

H
hanging herbs 115
hardening-off seedlings 87
hardiness 76–9
harvesting herbs 96, 106–7
herb gardens 83
hops 41
horseradish 25, 107, 127
  horseradish and bay leaf coating 140
hyssop 42

I
ice cubes, freezing herbs 110–11
iced tea 180
insect pests 98–9
invasive herbs 80

J, K
jasmine 42
juniper 43
  bay leaf, lovage, and juniper marinade 142
  sage, juniper, and bay leaf rub 137
kumquat 36

L
lavender 13, 44, 78
  lavender and lemon verbena tea 184
  lavender syrup 173
layering 91
leaf miners 98
lemon 37
  oregano, citrus, and rosemary rub 137
lemon balm 18, 45, 76, 80
  sage and lemon balm tea 184
lemongrass 38, 125
  lemongrass and chilli salsa 147
lime 37
  avocado, paprika, and lime salsa 148
linden flowers
  tilleul tea 183
liqueur, angelica 177
lovage 45
  bay leaf, lovage, and juniper marinade 142
  guacamole soup 168

M, N
manakeish 171
marigold, pot 28
marinades 142–5
marjoram 19, 55, 78
mayonnaise, herb 162
meadowsweet 38, 79
Mediterranean herbs 12–13
Middle Eastern herbs 14–15
mint 19, 48–9, 76, 79, 80
  coriander and mint coating 139
  mint and orange syrup 173
  mint dressing 156
  Moroccan mint tea 182
  yoghurt sauce with parsley and mint 163
Montpellier butter 133
Moroccan mint tea 182
mulches, weed control 95
mushrooms à la Grecque 145
muslin pouches 129
mustards 27, 80
myrtle 47
nasturtiums 72, 106

O
oils
  herb oil mixes 110
  rosemary oil 135
onions 20–1
orange 36
  citrus and basil marinade 143
  mint and orange syrup 173
oregano 9, 13, 16, 54, 80
  oregano butter 132
  oregano, citrus, and rosemary rub 137

P
parsley 9, 11, 15, 57
  chimichurri 163
  herb mayonnaise 162
  herb tabbouleh 152
  parsley, caper, and olive vinaigrette 157
  parsley, tarragon, and lemon thyme rub 136
  persillade 137
  sage and parsley coating 139
  sauce verte 161
  snail butter 133
  tarator soup 169

yoghurt sauce with parsley and mint 163
peas
  sorrel and pea soup 167
peppermint 49
  four-herb digestif tea 183
perennials, dividing 91
perilla 51
persillade 137
pestles and mortars 125
pesto, mixed herb 159
pests 98–9
pH levels, soil 85
pinching out 96
planning 80–3
planting 88–9
pots 80, 89, 92–3, 97
potting on 89
preparing herbs 122–7
propagating 90–1
pruning 96–7
purslane 58, 80

R
radicchio 33
rocambole 21
rocket 10, 39, 77
  dandelion, rocket, and flower salad 151
  rocket and mascarpone salsa 148
root cuttings 90
roots 88, 107
rose 60
rosehip tea 182
rosemary 12, 17, 62–3, 77
  oregano, citrus, and rosemary rub 137
  rosemary, garlic, and olive topping 171
  rosemary oil 135
rosemary beetles 99
rubs 136–7

S
sage 8, 13, 17, 64–5, 77
  fresh sage sauce 164
  sage and lemon balm tea 184
  sage and parsley coating 139
  sage, juniper, and bay leaf rub 137
salad burnet 67
salads 10–11, 151–5
salsas 147–9
sauce verte 161

sauces 161–5
savory 17, 68
scarifying seeds 86
seedlings, transplanting 87
seeds 86, 106, 116
shepherd's salad 153
slugs 98
smallage 25
smoked haddock, dilled 144
snail butter 133
snails 98
soil 79, 84–5
solarizing, weed control 94
sorrel 17, 61
  sorrel and pea soup 167
soups 167–9
sowing seeds 86
spearmint 15, 48
spring herb salad with goat's cheese 153
stem cuttings 90
stevia 67
storage 108–19
sumac 59
syrups 173

T
tabbouleh, herb 152
tarator soup 169
tarragon 11, 26
  cucumber with tarragon
    and cream 144
  parsley, tarragon, and lemon
    thyme rub 136
  tarragon butter 132
  tarragon vinegar 135
tea bags 181
teas 18–19, 178–85
thyme 9, 12, 15, 16, 70–1, 76
  fennel and thyme rub 136
  manakeish 171
  parsley, tarragon, and lemon
    thyme rub 136
  tarator soup 169
tilleul tea 183
tomatoes
  dill, watercress, caper, and
    tomato salsa 149
  warm tomato and garlic vinaigrette 157
toppings 171
transplanting seedlings 87

V
verbena, lemon 19, 22
  lavender and lemon verbena tea 184
vinaigrettes 157
vine weevils 99
vinegar, tarragon 135
violet, sweet 73, 79
  sweet violet tea 182
virus diseases 101

W, Y
walnuts
  tarator soup 169
watercress 50, 79
  dill, watercress, caper, and tomato
    salsa 149
  guacamole soup 168
  watercress butter 130
watering 92–3
weeds 94–5
wet soils 79
woodruff, sweet 18, 41
yoghurt sauce with parsley and mint 16

ACKNOWLEDGMENTS

Dorling Kindersley would like to thank Helena Caldon and Constance Novis for their editing, William Reavell, Peter Anderson, and Sarah Ashun for the beautiful photography, Nicky Collings for directing the photography, Alison Shackleton for the use of her garden, Jan Stevens, Bren Parkins-Knight, and Anna Burges-Lumsden for their recipe testing, Jane Lawrie for her food styling, Victoria Allen for prop styling, Mandy Earey for her design assistance, Lucy Boyd, Helen Kells, and Charlotte Senn at Petersham Nurseries for their stunning herb plantings, Emma Callery and Kajal Mistry for their editorial help, Sue Morony for proof-reading, Hilary Bird for creating the index, Romaine Werblow for her picture research, and the following for their herbs: Arne Herbs, Jekka's Herb Farm, The Perennial Nursery, Cotswold Garden Flowers, Plants4Presents, and Highdown Nursery.

Jeff Cox I would like to acknowledge and thank my herbal mentors: Lamar Bumbaugh, who showed me where the ginseng grows; Cyrus Hyde of Wellsweep Herb Farm, who increased my general knowledge of herbs; and especially the great chefs of Sonoma County, California, who continue to show me how to use the culinary herbs to tasty advantage. Thanks to all at DK and to Helena Caldon for her editing prowess.

Mary-Pierre Moine Thanks to the DK team and in particular Andrew Roff, Constance Novis, and Helena Caldon for their thoroughness, tact, and sense of humour. I'd also like to thank Philippa Davenport who helped my herb gardens over the years by giving me my first plot of sorrel, and my latest cutting of lovage.

All images © Dorling Kindersley
For further information see: www.dkimages.com